I0159224

HELL KNOW!

Eternal Torment or DESTRUCTION?

(Condensed Version)

Dirk Waren

Soaring Eagle Press

HELL KNOW! (Condensed Version)

Copyright © 2019 by Dirk Waren

All rights reserved. No original part of this book may be reproduced or transmitted in any form or by any means, electronic or mechanical, including photocopying, recording, or by any information storage and retrieval system, without the written permission of the Publisher, except where permitted by law.

Unless otherwise indicated, all Scripture quotations are taken from the Holy Bible, New International Version®. NIV®. Copyright © 1973, 1978, 1984, 2011 by the International Bible Society. Used by permission of Zondervan Bible Publishers.

Many NIV citations are from the 2011 Revised edition.

Other cited translations are listed in the **Bibliography**.

All underlining, italics and bracketed notes in scriptural citations are added by the author.

Pronominal references to Deity in this work are not always capitalized.

ISBN: 978-0-578-52964-6
PUBLISHED BY SOARING EAGLE PRESS
Youngstown

Printed in the United States of America

For the wages of sin is death,
but the gift of God is eternal life
in Christ Jesus our Lord.

- Romans 6:23

CONTENTS

Introduction

The Bible teaches that those who reject God's message of reconciliation and gift of eternal life will be cast into the lake of fire, which is described as "the second death." This is eternal damnation with no hope of redemption. The purpose of *HELL KNOW* is to examine the Holy Scriptures to determine the nature of this "second death."

There's absolutely no disputing that eternal damnation is a dreadful reality in Christian thought. We should take the Bible's repeated warnings of such seriously, and encourage others to do the same.

HELL KNOW is intended for anyone who has an interest in finding out what the Bible plainly and consistently teaches about human damnation and related subjects. Whether you're a devoted Christian, a doubting believer, an agnostic, an atheist — or simply a fellow human being who disdains all such labeling — I welcome you on this journey of discovery.

1

HELL (DAMNATION):
What Does the Bible *Really* Teach?

Traditionally, the most prominent view on eternal damnation is that people cast into hell—the lake of fire—will suffer fiery conscious torment forever and ever. Depicting the horrors of this belief was a favorite subject with artists in medieval times, resulting in all manner of ghastly portraits of people suffering unending agony. Some have since tried to modify this position a bit, suggesting a more metaphorical view—that the unending pain refers to the mental anguish of eternal loss and "separation from God"—but it makes no appreciable difference as both views involve the notion of eternal torment.

This may be the traditionally prominent view of human damnation, but is it *biblical?* That is, do the Judeo-Christian Scriptures *really* teach it? Will the multitudes of people who reject God, and hence are rejected by God, really be subjected to *never-ending torment—* with no merciful pause to their misery?

One might contend that it is heretical to even question such a long-standing, widely-accepted teaching, but if this doctrine is truly scriptural then its proponents have no need to worry. Furthermore, all doctrines, no matter how traditional or popular, must be questioned in light of what the Bible clearly teaches; for it's the God-breathed Scriptures alone that we must look to for truth, not popularity or religious tradition. This is the theological principle of *sola scriptura*, Latin for "by Scripture alone," which maintains that the Bible is the final authority regarding all judgments of Christian doctrine and practice.

Due to this sound principle many traditional doctrines and practices have proven to be false over the years and have been corrected or discarded. It goes without saying that it's a positive thing for Christians to periodically reevaluate their beliefs and practices because it helps prevent Christendom from straying from the biblical model. Since reevaluating official Church teachings is very much a part of Christian heritage, and is indeed a healthy practice, there should be no problem here in entertaining the possibility that Church tradition may be in error with this belief of perpetual roasting torment.

Eternal Torture: The Silent Subject of the Church

I read in a major news magazine that the teaching of hell as eternal torture has all but disappeared from the pulpit ministry in both mainline and evangelical churches. Why is this so? Why are Christians who are committed to this doctrine so reluctant to openly and honestly preach it? Why do they mask what they really believe by saying that the unredeemed will ultimately "perish" or be "destroyed" or suffer eternal "separation from God"? Yes, you'll hear 'hell' thrown around now and then, but you'll rarely, if ever, hear anyone explain what he or she *really* means by the term—suffering fiery conscious torment forever and ever with no merciful respite from the agony.

If this is true, why is everyone so timid about spelling it out loud and clear? The answer is obvious: *They're ashamed of it.* They're ashamed of it because, as Clark Pinnock aptly put it, the doctrine of eternal torture makes God out to be morally worse than Hitler "who maintains an everlasting Auschwitz for his enemies whom he does not even allow to die. How can one love a God like that? I suppose one might be afraid of Him, but could we love and respect Him? Would we want to strive to be like Him in His mercilessness?" (149). Let's be honest here and tell it like it is: The doctrine of never-ending roasting torment makes God out to be a cruel, unjust, merciless monster. Who would possibly want to accept salvation from such a God?

Although there are many good reasons for questioning this teaching, the most important reason is the simple fact that the Bible does not teach it. Contrary to the loud claims of its staunch supporters, it is *not* a scriptural doctrine; and this is being realized by a growing number of biblically faithful Christians today. The Bible offers strong, irrefutable evidence to any unbiased reader that hell, the lake of fire, signifies literal ***everlasting destruction*** for ungodly people,[1] not eternal conscious torment.

This is the main reason why so many Christians of all persuasions are embracing the doctrine of everlasting destruction not because they're "going liberal" as supporters of eternal torment claim. It's a case of going *biblical,* not going liberal.

For clear proof that literal everlasting destruction is what the Bible really teaches, let us simply turn to the pages of Scripture; after all, a thorough, honest study of the Bible will always reveal the truth.

Life and Death: The Two Polar Opposites

The apostle Paul summed up the whole matter of people's reward for sin when he wrote:

---

[1] This view is often referred to as "conditional immortality" or "annihilationism," but I prefer "everlasting destruction," "literal destruction" or "destructionism" based on 2 Thessalonians 1:9 and numerous other passages. I consequently refer to it in these terms throughout this study.

> For the wages of sin is <u>death</u>, but the gift of God
> is <u>eternal life</u> through Christ Jesus our Lord.
> **Romans 6:23**

Could it be stated any plainer? The wages for sin is shown to be death; and eternal life is a gift from God, not something people already have. This is consistently expressed from Genesis to Revelation, notice:

> "Enter through the narrow gate, for wide is the gate and broad the road that leads to <u>destruction</u> and many enter through it. But small is the gate and narrow the road that leads to <u>life</u>, and only a few find it."
> **Matthew 7:13-14**

> "For God so loved the world that he gave his one and only Son, that whoever believes in him shall not <u>perish</u> but have <u>eternal life</u>."
> **John 3:16**

> For if you live according to the sinful nature, you will <u>die</u>; but if by the spirit you put to death the misdeeds of the body, you will <u>live</u>.
> **Romans 8:13**

> The one who sows to please the sinful nature from that nature will reap <u>destruction</u>; the one who sows to please the spirit, from the spirit will reap <u>eternal life</u>.
> **Galatians 6:8**

> The LORD <u>preserves</u> all who love Him,
> but all the wicked He will <u>destroy</u>.
> **Psalm 145:20** (NKJV)

> The truly righteous man attains <u>life</u>,
> but he who pursues evil goes to his <u>death</u>.
> **Proverbs 11:19**

All these passages clearly describe the two separate destinies of the righteous and the unrighteous. The "righteous" are people who are in right-standing with God because they've accepted his sacrifice for their sins while the "unrighteous" are those who are not in-right-standing with their Creator because they've rejected his offer of salvation.[2] The former will inherit eternal life whereas the latter will reap the wages of sin and be destroyed.

Yet those who adhere to the eternal torture doctrine mysteriously don't accept this blatantly clear biblical truth. They don't believe the two polar opposites are life and death; they believe the two polar opposites are eternal life in heavenly bliss and eternal life in burning torment. Sounds ridiculous, doesn't it? They may not phrase it in such an honest manner, but this is what they actually believe when you spell it out.

Life and Immortality—Only Available through the Gospel

The offer to receive eternal life as opposed to suffering everlasting destruction is the core message of the gospel of Christ, as plainly expressed in this passage:

> **But it** [God's grace] **has now been revealed through the appearing of our Savior, Christ Jesus, who has destroyed death <u>and has brought life and immortality to light through the gospel</u>."**
> **2 Timothy 1:10**

---

[2] Please don't misinterpret this description of people as "righteous." Our *own* righteousness apart from Christ is as "filthy rags" in God's holy sight (Isaiah 64:6). To become in right-standing with God we must let go of our fleshly 'righteousness' in acceptance of God's "gift of righteousness," which comes via spiritual regeneration through Christ (see Romans 5:17 and 2 Corinthians 5:21). This is *positional* righteousness. *Practical* righteousness naturally occurs as the believer learns to put off the "old self"—the flesh—and live according to his or her new nature, which is "created to be **like God** in **true righteousness** and holiness" (Ephesians 4:22-24).

Notice that life and immortality are *only available for people through the gospel*. What exactly is "the gospel?" The gospel literally means "good news." Its main message is summed up in the famous passage John 3:16: "For God so loved the world that he gave his one and only Son that whoever believes in him shall not perish but have eternal life." Note, again, what is clearly being contrasted in both of these passages: In John 3:16 *perish* is contrasted with the gift of *eternal life*. In 2 Timothy 1:10 *death* is contrasted with both *immortality* and *life*, which are said to be made available through the gospel. If the eternal torture doctrine were true, these verses would be contrasting eternal life and eternal life being tortured, or immortality and immortality in fiery torment. I realize this sounds absurd, but the Bible would certainly speak in such honest, blatant terms if this teaching were true. Does anyone seriously think that God would be misleading or ambiguous about such an important issue in his Holy Word—the everlasting fate of people who reject the gospel of reconciliation?

The reason the Bible doesn't speak in such ludicrous terms is because the doctrine of eternal torment in not a biblical teaching. The above passage, 2 Timothy 1:10, makes it plain that until Christ was raised for our justification, the power of death was *not* destroyed and therefore immortality was not available to us—*life* was not available to us. This is because we are all sinners (see Romans 3:23 and Ecclesiastes 7:20) and consequently all deserve death, "for the wages of sin is death." God cannot overlook this because he is perfectly just. One person cannot pay the penalty for another because both are sinful and deserve death. The only way we can escape this imminent death penalty is if a sinless person, who does not deserve death, dies in our place.

So what did God do? Because he so loved the world and didn't want anyone to perish, he gave his Son as a sin sacrifice in order that we may have the gift of eternal life. The difference between wages and a gift is that wages are earned while a gift is free. Jesus paid the death penalty that we've all earned so that we can have the free gift of eternal life. The LORD did this so that we could fellowship with him forever instead of reaping the wages of sin, which is death.

This fact that God Himself wants to have a relationship with us explains why the gospel is also referred to as "the message of reconciliation" (2 Corinthians 5:17-21). 'Reconciliation' means to turn from enmity to friendship. The gospel is good news indeed because, not only does it grant eternal life to those who accept it, but, it simultaneously enables us to have a *relationship* with the Creator of the universe!

Notice what the Bible declares will happen to those who reject the gospel:

> **"Whoever believes in the Son has eternal life, but whoever rejects the Son <u>will not see life</u>, for God's wrath remains on him."**
>
> **John 3:36**

The passage could not be plainer: Those who reject the Son *"will not see life."* God's Word is absolute, and this is an absolute statement: Those who reject Jesus Christ will not see any life at all. This includes even a pathetic life in roasting agony for all eternity. Such people will be justly-but-mercifully put to death, absolute death, for this is the wages of their actions. But our loving Creator doesn't want anyone to perish like this; He has provided a way to eternal life through his Son, Jesus Christ.

Do you see the simple, beautiful, clear message of the gospel here? God is just trying to save his beloved fallen creation, humanity, from sin and the wages thereof. Ezekiel 18:32 reveals the heart of God on the matter: " 'For I take no pleasure in the **death** of anyone,' declares the Sovereign LORD, 'Repent **and live!**' "

Jesus Taught Everlasting Destruction

Didn't Jesus preach that those who reject the gospel and refuse to repent will suffer never-ending torment in hell? Many ministers adamantly claim this, but what did the Messiah *actually say* as recorded in the Bible? Let's observe what Christ himself taught on the issue starting with a statement we've already looked at:

> **"Enter through the narrow gate. For wide and broad is the road that <u>leads to destruction</u> and many enter through it. But small is the gate and narrow the road that <u>leads to life</u>, and only a few find it."**
>
> **Matthew 7:13-14**

Seriously, how much clearer could the Lord possibly be? Destruction is the fate that awaits the "many" who will be thrown into the lake of fire, not perpetual undying agony in flames of torment. And notice, again, that this is **in contrast** to life that will be granted to the "few."

Christ repeatedly made this clear. Consider, for example, his simple statement, "Unless you repent, you will all likewise perish" (Luke 13:3,5 NASB). This mirrors Jesus' statement in John 3:16 regarding the fact that those who believe in him "… shall not perish, but have eternal life." "Perish" in both of these passages is *not* referring to the death we all must face at the end of this present earthly life. No, Jesus is obviously referring to a perishing that those who believe in him will not have to suffer—**the second death**, which takes place on the Day of Judgment when the damned are cast into the lake of fire. Revelation 20:11-15 verifies this; verses 14-15 state: "The lake of fire is the second death. If anyone's name was not found written in the book of life, he was thrown into the lake of fire."

What will happen to these people when they experience this "second death"? Jesus solemnly declared:

> **"Do not be afraid of those who kill the body but cannot kill the soul. Rather, be afraid of the One [God] who can <u>destroy both soul and body in hell</u>."** [3]
>
> **Matthew 10:28**

---

[3] "Hell" in this verse is translated from the Greek word *Gehenna,* which is an illustrative reference to the lake of fire. We'll examine *Gehenna* in the next chapter.

Christ explicitly informs us what God will do to unrepentant sinful people on the Day of Judgment: He will destroy both soul and body in the lake of fire, his chosen instrument of destruction.

Jesus is dealing specifically here with the subject of the second death and yet he says absolutely nothing about spending eternity in undying roasting torment. If this were true Jesus would tell us to "fear the One who is able to *preserve* the soul in hell." But this is not what he taught. Christ didn't teach it because it is not a biblical doctrine. Religion may teach it, but the Bible does not. God is going to unenthusiastically issue out the wages of sin and justly destroy the unrighteous, not sadistically torture them forever. Scripture clearly says:

> **There is only one lawgiver and judge, the One [God] who is able to <u>save</u> and <u>destroy</u>.**
> **James 4:12**

You see, God is going to do one of two things with people: He's either going to save them, that is, grant eternal life to those who respond favorably to his love and gracious gift of life, or he's going to justly-but-mercifully destroy them. He may or may not be the one who personally executes this sentence, but he's certainly the One who *authorizes* it. In this sense, at least, it is indeed God Himself who destroys the ungodly.

This fact that God is either going to save or destroy people based upon their freewill decision to accept or reject the gospel is clearly conveyed in this verse from Hebrews:

> **But we are not of those who shrink back and are <u>destroyed</u>, but of those who believe and are <u>saved</u>.**
> **Hebrews 10:39**

"Those who believe" will be granted eternal life and saved from the second death whereas those who do not will be destroyed, both soul and body, in the lake of fire. Why do religionists insist on making such a simple truth so complicated and perverse?

"Destroy both Soul and Body" as in Complete Incineration

We've viewed some pretty clear biblical texts plainly stating that unrepentant sinners will ultimately perish and be destroyed. Let's now dig a little deeper and trace these words to the original language in which they were written.

The words "perish" (from John 3:16 and Luke 13:3,5) and "destroy" (from Matthew 10:28 and James 4:12) are both English translations of the Greek word *apollumi (ah-POHL-loo-mee),* which literally means "to destroy utterly" or "to perish."

Apollumi is used most often in the Bible simply in reference to the natural death we all must experience at the end of our present lives—the *first* death. Notice, for example, how *apollumi* is used by the disciples when a squall threatened their lives as they crossed the Sea of Galilee:

> **Jesus was in the stern, sleeping on a cushion. The disciples woke him and said to him, "Teacher, don't you care if we <u>drown</u>** *(apollumi)?"*
>
> **Mark 4:38**

As you can see, *apollumi* here simply refers to death by drowning. *Apollumi* is used 26 other times in the New Testament in reference to the first death. Likewise, Homer, in his epics of Greek antiquity, used *apollumi* chiefly of death in battle.

The apostles, like Jesus, used this same word, *apollumi,* in reference to the *second* death—the eternal fate of the ungodly:

> **For the message of the cross is foolishness to those who are <u>perishing</u>** *(apollumi);* **but to those who are being saved, it is the power of God.**
>
> **1 Corinthians 1:18**

They <u>perish</u> *(apollumi)* **because they refuse to love the truth and be saved.**

2 Thessalonians 2:10b

He is patient with you, not wanting anyone to <u>perish</u> *(apollumi)*, **but everyone to come to repentance.**

2 Peter 3:9b

All these passages are referring to what will happen at the second death and yet, again, there is mysteriously no mention of eternal roasting in conscious torment. In view of such blatantly clear biblical evidence, how can adherents of eternal torture possibly maintain their view? Their theory is that, in all these cases, the Greek word *apollumi* does not literally mean "to destroy utterly" or "to perish," but that the idea is "not extinction, but ruin, loss, not of being, but of well-being" (Vine 164/Pearlman 387). This theory is a good example of trying to make the Scriptures line up with one's favored doctrine rather than lining up one's doctrine with what the Scriptures literally teach.

There are a number of reasons for rejecting this theory. For one, the Bible itself provides definitive proof of what *apollumi* means when used in reference to the second death: The word is used by Christ in Luke 17:29[4] to describe the destruction of Sodom and Gomorrah: " 'But the day Lot left Sodom, fire and sulfur rained down from heaven and **destroyed** *(apollumi)* them all.' "

Since *apollumi* is used to describe this destruction, the question must be asked: how were the cities of Sodom & Gomorrah and their inhabitants destroyed? Was the well-being of these cities merely ruined? No, Genesis 19:24-28 verifies that they were **completely burned to ashes**. This includes all the people in them, all the animals, and even the vegetation—in fact, all the land of the entire plain that these cities occupied! Peter also verifies this:

---

[4] Jesus no doubt spoke in Hebrew or Aramaic during his earthly ministry but Luke, inspired by the Holy Spirit, had his words recorded in Koine Greek.

> **if he** [God] **condemned the cities of Sodom and Gomorrah <u>by burning them to ashes</u>...**
>
> **2 Peter 2:6a**

"Ashes" here is the Greek word *tephroo (tef-ROH-oh)*, which means "to incinerate, i.e. consume" (Strong 71); and *apollumi* is the Greek word used to describe this absolute incineration as shown above in Luke 17:29. My point is that *apollumi*, in this case, refers to utter destruction and perishing in the sense of **complete incineration**. The idea "not extinction, but ruin, loss, not of being, but of well-being" does not fit at all because the well-being of Sodom and Gomorrah wasn't merely ruined; these cities were completely and finally destroyed by incineration—forever obliterated!

But there's more: Peter goes on to say that this utter incineration of Sodom and Gomorrah is an *example* of what will happen to the ungodly:

> **if he** [God] **condemned the cities of Sodom and Gomorrah by burning them to ashes <u>and</u> made them <u>an example</u> <u>of what is going to happen to the ungodly</u>;**
>
> **2 Peter 2:6**

We know that Peter is specifically referring to what will happen to the ungodly on Judgment Day when they're thrown into the lake of fire—that is, the second death—because this will be the only time that all the ungodly will experience a fate comparable to the judgment of Sodom and Gomorrah.

If the incineration of Sodom and Gomorrah is a true and trustworthy example of what will happen to the ungodly when they suffer the second death, then we must conclude that the ungodly will, in fact, be incinerated. And if it is certain that the Greek word *apollumi* refers to absolute incineration in reference to the destruction of Sodom and Gomorrah, then it naturally follows that *apollumi* must also refer to absolute incineration when it is used in reference to the second death because **the incineration of Sodom and Gomorrah is an *example* of the second death**.

So, as you can see, by following the hermeneutical rule of allowing Scripture to interpret Scripture we have a clear understanding that the Greek word *apollumi,* when used in reference to the second death (e.g. Matthew 10:28), refers to nothing other than complete and final destruction. Hence the dubious theory of "not extinction, but ruin, loss, not of being, but of well-being" is proven false.

As if this weren't enough, there's much more scriptural proof that *apollumi* refers to literal destruction when applied to the second death. To start with, there are many other biblical words, besides *apollumi,* which describe the second death strictly in terms of complete and irreversible death and destruction. Let's look at these words.

" The Wages of Sin is <u>Death</u>," Not Eternal Torment

Let's begin with the Greek word *thanatos (THAYN-ah-tohs).* This word simply means "death" (Strong 35), the express opposite of life according to Romans 8:38, and therefore the cessation of conscious existence. *Thanatos* is most often used in the Bible simply in reference to the death that all human beings must one day experience—the first death (e.g. Acts 23:29). The first death therefore refers *at least* to the cessation of conscious existence in the physical realm.

Thanatos is also used in reference to the second death—the destruction of both soul and body in the lake of fire. In fact the Greek word translated as "death" in the phrase "the second death" **is** *thanatos.* For instance, " 'He who overcomes will not be hurt at all by the second death *(thanatos)'* " (Revelation 2:11). The verse refers to those who "overcome," meaning all true believers (see 1 John 5:4). Genuine believers will not be hurt at all by the second death. The second death has no power over spiritually born-again believers because they've been saved from God's wrath through Christ's death, burial and resurrection. That's why Jesus said:

> **"I tell you the truth, if anyone keeps my word he will never see <u>death</u>** *(thanatos).* **"**
>
> **John 8:51**

This is obviously not referring to the first death; after all, Christians who have faithfully "kept his word" have been physically dying for two thousand years. No, this is a reference to the *second* death. Jesus' promise is that true believers will never experience the destruction of the second death in the lake of fire. This coincides perfectly with what Christ said in John 3:16: that those who believe in him "shall not perish but have eternal life."

As important as it is to point out what the Bible says, it's sometimes important to point out what the Bible does not say as well. Notice that Jesus does *not* say, "if anyone keeps my word he will never see eternal life in conscious torment." Jesus doesn't say this, does he? No, he simply states that those who keep his word will never see death—the second death—the destruction of soul and body in the lake of fire.

The second death is the ultimate consequence of sin according to the Bible: "The wages of sin is death" (Romans 6:23), "sin… leads to death" (Romans 6:16), and sin will "result in death" (Romans 6:21). "Death" in all these verses is the Greek word *thanatos,* and they all refer to the ultimate penalty of sin—the second death.

James 1:14-15 clearly says that "sin, when it is full-grown, gives birth to death *(thanatos)."* Note that sin ultimately gives birth to death, not life in everlasting fiery torment. This is emphasized again later in James:

> **You should know that whoever brings back a sinner from wandering will save that sinner's soul from <u>death</u>** *(thanatos).*
>
> **James 5:20** (NRSV)

We observe here that if a person is not brought back from the error of a sinful lifestyle, their soul will die! When did Jesus say a soul would die and by whom? He said that God Himself would "destroy both soul and body in hell" (Matthew 10:28). So we know this verse is definitely a reference to the second death as well. Notice that a sinner's soul is not saved from never-ending roasting torment, but from death. The Bible's repeatedly clear on this matter.

" Their Destiny is <u>Destruction</u>"

The Greek word *apoleia (ah-POHL-lee-ah),* which is the noun form of *apollumi,* refers to utter destruction and is often used in reference to the eternal fate of the ungodly, i.e. the second death. This is the case with the aforementioned Matthew 7:13-14 where Jesus said "wide is the gate and broad is the road that leads to **destruction** *(apoleia)* and many enter through it." Jesus spoke of this destruction in direct contrast to the "life" that would be granted to the righteous "few;" so obviously *apoleia* **is the direct opposite of life**, namely death.

In 2 Peter 3:7 *apoleia* is used to describe the destruction of the second death:

> **By the same word the present heavens and earth are reserved for fire, being kept for <u>the day of judgment and destruction</u>** *(apoleia)* **<u>of ungodly men</u>.**
>
> **2 Peter 3:7**

The Day of Judgment is the day when ungodly people will suffer everlasting destruction. This is their "eternal punishment" as God destroys "both soul and body in hell" (please notice that I said "eternal punishment" and not "eternal punish*ing*"; there's a difference).

This is the ultimate destiny of God's enemies as Paul verifies in Philippians 3:18-19: "For, as I have told you before and now say again even with tears, many live as enemies of the cross of Christ. Their destiny is **destruction** *(apoleia)."* As such, the Bible repeatedly refers to God's enemies as "doomed to **destruction** *(apoleia)"* or "prepared for **destruction** *(apoleia)"* (see John 17:12, 2, Thessalonians 2:3 and Romans 9:22).

Apoleia is also translated as "destroyed" in reference to the eternal fate of God's enemies: "...they will be **destroyed** *(apoleia)"* (Philippians 1:28), "we are not of those who shrink back and are **destroyed** *(apoleia)"* (Hebrews 10:39).

You see? The eternal destiny of ungodly people who reject God's love in Christ is **destruction**. In other words, they will ultimately be destroyed. Seriously, how much plainer could the Bible be on the subject?

" They will be Punished with Everlasting Destruction"

The Greek word *olethros (OL-eth-ross),* which means "destruction" (Vine 165), is used by Paul to describe the eternal punishment of the second death:

> **In flaming fire taking vengeance on them that know not God, and that obey not the gospel of the Lord Jesus Christ: [9] Who shall be punished with everlasting <u>destruction</u> *(olethros)* from the presence of the Lord, and from the glory of his power.**
> **2 Thessalonians 1:8-9** (KJV)

The first part of this passage shows that God will punish those who reject the gospel and verse 9 reveals exactly what this punishment will be: **everlasting destruction**. This obviously refers to destruction that lasts forever and not to an endless process of destroying without ever quite destroying, as supporters of eternal torment weakly argue. After all, to perpetually destroy without ever destroying isn't really destruction because the destruction never actually takes place. This would be everlasting torment but not everlasting destruction.

Adherents of eternal torture also argue that if, in fact, "destruction" refers to complete extinction it would not be necessary to describe it as "everlasting." Yet the reason the destruction is described as everlasting is obvious: "Everlasting destruction" is a reference to the second death. The second death is different from the first death in that everyone is resurrected from the first death to face judgment whereas no one is resurrected from the second death. It is a death that lasts forever—an *"everlasting* destruction"—destruction that lasts forever.

The passage goes on to reveal that this everlasting destruction shall proceed "from the presence of the Lord, and from the glory of his power." This is further evidence that it is God Himself, the supreme authority and judge, who will execute the everlasting destruction of the second death.

The New International Version translates verse 9 as "They will be punished with everlasting destruction and shut out from the presence of the Lord and from the majesty of his power." This translation is acceptable as well, as both versions could be read together as such: God will punish the ungodly with everlasting destruction which proceeds from his presence and, consequently, removes and eradicates them from his presence forever.

To shed a bit more light on the meaning of *olethros,* the Greek word translated as "destruction" in this text, the verb form of this word, *olothreuo (ol-oth-RYOO-oh),* is used in Hebrews 11:28 in reference to the death angel—"the destroyer"—who slew all the firstborn of Egypt (see Exodus 12:29). So we're talking about destruction in the sense of *slaying* here, which will be executed on "the day of judgment and destruction of ungodly men" (2 Peter 3:7).

"If You Live according to the Sinful Nature you will <u>Die</u>"

Let's examine yet another biblical word used to describe the second death, the Greek word *apothnesko (ap-oth-NAYS-koh).*

Apothnesko simply means "to die off" (Strong 14)—to cease to live—and is exclusively translated as "die," "died," "dies," "dead," "dying" and "death" in the New International Version of the Bible. Unsurprisingly, *apothnesko* most often refers to the death all humans and animals must face at the end of their earthly sojourn. For instance, *apothnesko* is used in Matthew 8:32 in reference to pigs that "died in the water" and also in Revelation 8:9 and 16:3 in reference to millions of sea creatures that "died." *Apothnesko* obviously refers to the utter cessation of life in these cases. The word is also used myriad of times in reference to the (first) death of human beings (e.g. Acts 9:37).

With this understanding, observe how *apothnesko* is used in reference to the *second* death in a passage already briefly viewed:

> **For if you live according to the sinful nature you will <u>die</u>** *(apothnesko);* **but if by the Spirit you put to death the misdeeds of the body, you will <u>live</u>.**
> **Romans 8:13**

Those who embrace sin and reject God will one day reap the wages of their actions; they will die. We know this isn't a reference to the first death because even those who "by the Spirit… put to death the misdeeds of the body" will also one day die (unless they're raptured). So this is a definite reference to the *second* death where God will "destroy both soul and body in hell."

Here's a case where Jesus used *apothnesko* in reference to both the first death *and* the second death:

> **"I am the bread of life. [49] Your forefathers ate manna in the desert, yet they <u>died</u>** *(apothnesko).* **[50] But here is the bread that comes down from heaven, which a man may eat and not <u>die</u>** *(apothnesko).* **[51] I am the living bread that came down from heaven. If anyone eats of this bread, he will <u>live forever</u>."**
> **John 6:48-51a**

In this passage Christ is likening himself to the "bread of life... that comes down from heaven" in comparison to the earthly "bread," manna, that God miraculously provided the Israelites when they were wandering in the desert (Exodus 16:15,31).

As you can see, *apothnesko* appears twice in this passage. The first time, in verse 49, it's obviously used in reference to the death that all people must face at the end of their earthly lives, **the first death**. Jesus points out that the Israelite forefathers who partook of manna—the earthly "bread"—died. The second time *apothnesko* appears (verse 50) it is used in reference to **the second death** as Jesus declares that those who partake of him—the heavenly bread of life—will not die, but "will live forever" (verse 51).

We know for certain that Christ is not referring to the first death in verse 50 because even people who partake of the bread of heaven—that is, accept Christ as Lord—will one day die. No, Jesus is referring to another death—the second death.

We could sum up this passage as such: Those who partake of Jesus Christ, the heavenly bread of life, will not suffer the second death, but will live forever.

Observe a very similar statement by Jesus in which *apothnesko* is also used:

> **Jesus said to her, "I am the resurrection and the life, he who believes in me will live even though he <u>dies</u>** *(apothnesko);* **²⁶ and whoever lives and believes in me will never <u>die</u>** *(apothnesko).* **Do you believe this?"**
>
> **John 11:25-26**

Apothnesko appears twice in this passage as well; and, like the other one, the first time it is used in reference to **the first death** and the second time in reference to **the second death**.

For verification, note that Jesus says in verse 25 that those who believe in him will live even though they die. All Jesus is saying is that, because he is the resurrection and the life, those who believe in him, even though they will die (that is, suffer the first death), they'll be resurrected unto eternal life. Jesus spoke of this resurrection when he declared:

> **"... a time is coming when all who are in their graves will hear his voice [29] and come out—those who have done good will <u>rise to live</u>, and those who have done evil will <u>rise to be condemned</u>."**
>
> **John 5:28-29**

We see two classes of people referred to in this passage: "Those who have done good" will rise to live. This is referring to the resurrection unto eternal life spoken of in Daniel 12:2. Revelation 20:6 states that "the second death has no power over" the people who partake of this resurrection. This explains why Jesus says in John 11:26 (above) that believers "will never die"—they will not suffer the second death. By contrast, the other class of people—"those who have done evil"—will rise to be judged and condemned. Condemned to what? Condemned to the second death where Christ said God will "destroy both soul and body."

As we have observed from the passages examined in this section—Romans 8:13, John 6:50 and John 11:26—the Greek word *apothnesko,* which means "to die," is used to describe the second death. Why? Obviously because the people thrown into the lake of fire on Judgment Day will die. Certainly there will be a period of conscious suffering as with any execution—however long or brief—and no doubt this suffering will be meted out as divine justice requires for each individual, but the final, everlasting outcome for people thrown into the lake of fire is that they will die. If this were not the case the above passages wouldn't use *apothnesko* to describe the second death.

The Language of Destruction

Up to this point we've plainly seen that the usual, basic meaning of the Greek word *apollumi*—"to perish" or "destroy utterly"—is

backed up by many other biblical words that likewise describe the second death strictly in terms of literal death and complete destruction.

Let's briefly review what Christ and the apostles plainly taught will happen to ungodly people when they suffer the second death. They taught that:

- the ungodly would **die** (John 11:26 & Romans 8:13),
- that they would experience **death** (John 8:51, Romans 6:23 & James 5:20),
- that **destruction** would occur (Matthew 7:13 & 2 Peter 3:7),
- that both their souls and bodies would be **destroyed** (Matthew 10:28 & James 4:12),
- and that they would **perish** (John 3:16 & 2 Peter 3:9).

So there you have it in a nutshell—Jesus and the apostles' description of the second death: **die**, **death**, **destruction**, **destroy** and **perish**. We could appropriately describe these terms as the "language of destruction." This "language of destruction" is consistently used to describe the eternal fate of the ungodly in the Bible; not the language of eternal conscious torment, not the language of "eternal separation from God," not the language of "ruin, loss, not of being, but of well-being," but the **language of destruction**.

If the eternal fate of unrepentant sinners is to be some sort of perpetual life or existence in separation from God in roasting misery and torment, God would have said so. He could have used words that basically mean "separation from God," "existence in torment," or "life in misery." But he didn't do this. No, he consistently used words which have for their general, usual, or basis meaning "die," "death," "destruction," "destroy," and "perish." If language means anything at all, we have no choice but to conclude that the second death will be a literal death—utter, awful, complete and final.

As if this consistent usage of "the language of destruction" in the Scriptures isn't evidence enough, the Bible gives numerous easy-to-understand *examples* to support it. Let's look at these examples…

2
—

BIBLICAL EXAMPLES
of Everlasting Destruction

Let's now focus on biblical *examples* of literal everlasting destruction that **back-up** the numerous passages which blatantly state that unredeemed people will be destroyed in the lake of fire and not suffer never-ending roasting torment, such as Matthew 10:28, 2 Thessalonians 1:9 and 2 Peter 3:7.

The Example of Gehenna: "Hell"

We'll begin with the very word "hell" itself. There is only one biblical word translated as "hell" that refers to the lake of fire and is therefore relevant to the final disposition of ungodly people: *Gehenna (geh-HEN-nah)*. Gehenna is the Greek form of the Hebrew *Ge-Hinnom*, which literally means "the Valley of Hinnom" *(HIN-uhm)*. The Hinnom Valley was also referred to as *Topheth (TOH-feth)*, meaning "a place to be spat on or abhorred." It borders Jerusalem to the south and can easily be located on close-up Bible maps of Jerusalem. This was the valley Jesus was referring to when he said, "...be afraid of the One who can destroy both soul and body in **hell** *(Gehenna)."* Why would Jesus use this ravine located outside the walls of Jerusalem as an *example* of the lake of fire and the destruction that will take place there on Judgment Day?

To answer, let me briefly inform you about Gehenna's infamous history: The worst of Judah's kings practiced pagan worship in the Hinnom Valley, with child sacrifice being a particularly offensive aspect of this "worship" (2 Kings 16:3 & 21:6). The valley apparently became a fiery disposal dump for 185,000 Assyrian warriors slain by the LORD (see 2 Kings 19:35, Isaiah 30:33 and 37:36), and, later, it would overflow with Israelite corpses as well when God judged Judah for its sins. Consequently Gehenna became known as "the Valley of Slaughter" (Jeremiah 7:30-34 & 19:2-13). Note incidentally that Gehenna was known as "the Valley of **Slaughter**" and not "the Valley of Eternal Torture," an important difference. Needless to say, long before Jesus' earthly ministry Gehenna had a negative image of sinful rebellion, fire and death.

After righteous King Josiah desecrated Gehenna as part of his godly reforms (2 King 23:10), the valley became the constantly smoking trash dump of Jerusalem, which is what it was at the time of Christ. As a hygienic incinerator, Gehenna's fires were kept burning in order to **burn up** the refuse thrown in—trash, garbage, animal carcasses, corpses of despised criminals and vanquished enemies. As would be natural in such an environment, worms or maggots bred freely and preyed upon the remains. As such, whatever was not burned up in the fires would be devoured by maggots.

James Tabor, a professor of religious studies, commented about Gehenna on A&E's *Mysteries of the Bible* segment "Heaven and Hell":

"I've been to hell; many times I've been there and walked through it. It's a valley on the south side of Jerusalem that anciently was a despicable place of child sacrifice; it's mentioned in the Hebrew Bible a number of times. **In Jesus' day it was a garbage dump and so the fire was always burning** *and the maggots working and dead animals were thrown in there. Today you walk out the Dung Gate and look down in the Valley of Hinnom—that's hell."*

Christ used this smoking garbage dump as a figure for the lake of fire when he said God will "destroy both soul and body in hell *(Gehenna)*" in Matthew 10:28. The question must be asked: Why did the Lord feel Gehenna would be a good example of the second death? **Because Gehenna was a certain symbol of destruction that all of his hearers readily understood.** We saw earlier how supporters of eternal torture argue that "destroy" only refers to a ruined condition, but this does not fit Jesus' usage of Gehenna as an example of the second death. Why? Because every cell of every body thrown into Gehenna was either burned up in fire or digested by worms; a body could not be destroyed anymore completely.

The implication of Gehenna is clear: Those who reject God's love in Christ become God's garbage and will consequently be disposed of in the LORD's incinerating "garbage dump," the lake of fire.

We cannot properly understand Christ's teaching about the lake of fire and eternal punishment without keeping in mind this picture of Gehenna. Rubbish was thrown into Gehenna for the purpose of **disposal and eradication** and, as such, the infamous ravine was a fitting figure for the second death.

These facts show that it's not really a good practice to translate Gehenna as "hell" in modern English Bibles. Why? Because the word 'hell' typically conjures up images based more on medieval mythology than on biblical fact (e.g. Dante's *Inferno*). The common image 'hell' provokes is that of people eternally roasting in fire pits while devils poke them with pitchforks. It's very comic booky. The biblical image of Gehenna is quite different in that the

Valley of Hinnom elicits the image of **ultimate disposal and eradication**. It would therefore be more accurate and informative to translate Gehenna as "the Valley of Hinnom" in biblical texts, even though it's a symbolic reference to the lake of fire and second death. For example, Matthew 10:28 should literally read: "'Do not be afraid of those who kill the body but cannot kill the soul. Rather, be afraid of the One [God] who can destroy both soul and body in the Valley of Hinnom.' "

When this is done we get the proper impression of **disposal and eradication** rather than that of never-ending fiery torture in a devil-ruled nether realm. Disposal and eradication is the impression Jesus endeavored to give.

The Examples of Weeds, Trees, Branches and Chaff

Jesus also used many examples of literal everlasting destruction in his parables to back-up his words and to illustrate that God would destroy the ungodly in the lake of fire, not torture them forever.

The Bible says that Christ spoke in parables to reveal "things hidden since the creation of the world" (Matthew 13:35). In other words, the Messiah used figurative tales as a means to reveal scriptural truths to the common people. In many of these stories natural things are used symbolically in order to explain principles of truth. For instance, the "ground" in The Parable of the Sower (Luke 8:1-15) represents a person's heart and "seed" represents the word of God. While these parables are easy-to-understand for those with spiritual discernment they simultaneously hide truth from arrogant fools, including sterile religionists, like the Pharisees (Matthew 13:10-15 & 1 Corinthians 2:14).

Let's observe a clear example of everlasting destruction contained in The Parable of the Weeds (or "Tares" in the KJV):

Jesus told them another parable: "The kingdom of heaven is like a man who sowed seed in his field. [25] But while everyone was sleeping, his enemy came and sowed weeds among the wheat, and went away. [26] When the wheat sprouted and formed heads, then the weeds also appeared. [27] The owner's servants came to him and said, 'Sir, didn't you sow good seed in your field? Where then did the weeds come from?' [28] 'An enemy did this,' he replied. The servants asked him, 'do you want us to go and pull them up?' [29] 'No,' he answered, 'because while you are pulling the weeds, you may root up the wheat with them. [30] Let both grow together until the harvest. At that time I will tell the harvesters: First collect <u>the weeds</u> and tie them in bundles <u>to be burned</u>; then gather the wheat and bring it into my barn.' "

Matthew 13:24-30

In verses 37-39 Jesus explains the symbolism of this parable: The owner of the field who sowed the good seed is Christ, the "field" is the world, the "wheat" is the righteous, the "weeds" are ungodly people while the "enemy" who sowed them is the devil, the "harvest" is the end of the age, and the "harvesters" are angels. After explaining this symbolism, the Lord says:

"As the weeds are pulled up and burned in the fire, <u>so will it be</u> at the end of the age."

Matthew 13:40

Christ is saying that *just as* weeds are burned in the fire in his story, **so it will be** with ungodly people—God's enemies—at the end of this age on Judgment Day.

When literal weeds are burned, they are **burned up**. Was Jesus using a wrong example here or did he mean what he said? The obvious answer is that he meant exactly what he said. When the ungodly are thrown into the lake of fire, they—like the weeds—will be burned up.

The above example of weeds is backed up by three similar examples used in the gospels. In Matthew 7:19 Jesus likened the ungodly to trees: "Every tree that does not bear good fruit is **cut down and thrown into the fire**." In John 15:6 he likened those who reject him to branches: "If anyone does not remain in me, he is like a branch that is thrown away and withers; such branches are picked up, **thrown into the fire and burned**." Similarly, in Luke 3:17 John the Baptist likened evildoers to chaff: "His [Jesus'] winnowing fork is in his hand to clear his threshing floor and to gather the wheat into his barn, but **he will BURN UP the chaff with unquenchable fire**."

In all these cases the "trees," "branches" and "chaff" represent ungodly people—God's enemies—and these combustible articles are to be "thrown [discarded] into fire and **burned**." Luke 3:17 even specifies that they will be **burned up**.

As with the Parable of the Weeds above, the "fire" in all these examples is, of course, a reference to the lake of fire. When the ungodly are thrown into the lake of fire, they—like the trees, branches and chaff—will be burned up.

As you can see, the Lord makes the issue of human damnation so simple and clear that even a child can understand it.

"Like Green Plants They Will Soon Die Away"

Let's look at some similar examples of literal destruction used elsewhere in Scripture:

> **[1] Do not fret because of evil men**
> **or be envious of those who do wrong;**
> **[2] for like the grass they will soon wither,**
> **like green plants they will soon die away.**
> **Psalm 37:1-2**

Notice how evil people are likened to grass that will ultimately wither and to green plants that will eventually **die away**.

Adherents of eternal torment would contend that this passage is referring to physical death in the here in now (the first death) and not to eternal death (the second death), but verses 9-13 refute this argument:

> ⁹ **For evil men will be cut off,**
>   **but those who hope in the LORD <u>will</u>**
>   <u>**inherit the land.**</u>
> ¹⁰ **A <u>little while and the wicked will be no more</u>;**
>   **though you look for them, <u>they will not be</u>**
>   <u>**found.**</u>
> ¹¹ <u>**But the meek will inherit the land**</u>
>   **and enjoy great peace.**
> ¹² **The wicked plot against the righteous**
>   **and gnash their teeth at them;**
> ¹³ **but the LORD laughs at the wicked**
>   **for he knows their <u>day</u> is coming.**
>   **Psalm 37:9-13**

These verses show that this is an eschatological passage—a text dealing with the ultimate fate of humankind and the world. Note how verse 9 refers to a time when evil people will ultimately be cut off, but "those who hope in the LORD" will inherit the land. Verse 11 further emphasizes that the meek will inherit the land and verse 29 adds an important detail, "the righteous will inherit the land and **dwell in it forever**." These two verses coincide with Jesus' statement in Matthew 5:5 that "the meek shall inherit the earth." Christ was of course referring to the new earth detailed in Revelation 21:1-5.

Biblically, we know that *all* evil people will not be cut off until "the day of judgment and destruction of ungodly men" (2 Peter 3:7 & Revelation 20:11-15). We also know that the meek or righteous will not inherit the earth forever until the new earth—"the home of righteousness"—is revealed (2 Peter 3:13).

Furthermore, observe verses 10 and 13: "A little while and the wicked will be **no more**... but the LORD laughs at the wicked for he knows their **day** is coming." Verse 10 refers to a time when all the wicked will be "no more" and the Bible clearly reveals that the only time this will become a reality is, again, "the day of judgment and destruction of ungodly men." This is why, according to verse 13, the LORD laughs at the wicked because "he knows their day is coming." What day? Why, the Day of Judgment, of course!

" They Will Vanish—Vanish Like Smoke"

With the understanding that Psalm 37 contains eschatological references, let's observe verse 20:

> But <u>the wicked will perish</u>:
>> The LORD's enemies will be like the beauty of the fields,
>> <u>they will vanish—vanish like smoke</u>.
>>> **Psalm 37:20**

Note the explicit proclamation that "the wicked will perish." It doesn't say the wicked will be consciously tormented in fire forever and ever, but that they will perish. The rest of the verse gives a natural illustration so that we'll understand this perishment: It likens God's enemies to "the beauty of the fields" that will be burned up. According to this unmistakable example, what will be the ultimate end of God's enemies? It says "they will **vanish— vanish like smoke**." I'm again compelled to ask, how much clearer could the Scriptures possibly be? The LORD's enemies will not perpetually exist in fiery conscious torment, they're going to be consumed by fire and go up in smoke.

A similar illustration is used in the New Testament:

> **Land that drinks in the rain often falling on it and that produces a crop useful to those for whom it is farmed receives the blessing of God. [8]But <u>land</u> that produces thorns and thistles is worthless and is in danger of being cursed. In the end it will be <u>burned</u>.**
>> **Hebrews 6:7-8**

The worthless "land" in verse 8 produces nothing but thorns and thistles and, as such, is a figurative reference to worthless counterfeit Christians who profess to know Christ but bear no fruit (see verses 4-6 for verification). By contrast, the land that produces a useful crop in verse 7 refers to fruit-bearing, faithful Christians. The productive "land" will receive the blessings of God, but notice what happens to the worthless land that produces thorns and thistles: "In the end it will be **burned**."

This example coincides with Jesus' two examples above: Every tree that does not bear good fruit will be cut down and thrown into the fire; every branch that bears no fruit is cut off the vine and thrown into the fire. Likewise, the worthless land that produces thorns and thistles will be **burned in the end**. The purpose for burning such a field is to destroy that which is useless, not to preserve it. In the same way, ungodly people who fail to bear good fruit will be destroyed, not preserved for eternal roasting misery.

"Bring Them Here and Kill Them in Front of Me"

Continuing with the examples of literal everlasting destruction that Christ used in his parables, let's look at The Parable of the Ten Minas:

> **...he went on to tell them a parable, because he was near Jerusalem and the people thought that the kingdom of God was going to appear at once. [12] He said: "A man of noble birth went to a distant country to have himself appointed as king and then to return. [13] So he called ten of his servants and gave them ten minas.[5] 'Put this money to work,' he said, 'until I come back.' [14]But his subjects hated him and sent a delegation after him to say, 'We don't want this man to be our king,' "**
>
> **Luke 19:11-14**

---

[5] One mina was equal to about three months' wages.

The symbolism is obvious: the "man of noble birth" refers to Jesus, the Son of God; the "distant country" where the man of noble birth goes to have himself appointed as king—and then return—is the world; the place he would return to is heaven; the subjects who hate the new monarch and reject his kingship are people in this world who love sin, hate the Messiah and reject his Lordship.

Now let's skip down to verse 27 and observe what the king in the parable—symbolizing Christ—said should be done to these subjects who hated him and rejected his reign:

> **'But those enemies of mine who did not want me to be king over them—bring them here and <u>kill them in front of me</u>.'**
>
> **Luke 19:27**

The king having the subjects who hated & rejected him brought before him is an obvious reference to The White Throne Judgment (Revelation 20:11-15), and possibly The Pre-Millennial Judgment of Christ as well (Matthew 25:31-46),[6] both cases in which those who reject Jesus as Lord will be thrown into the lake of fire to suffer the second death. Notice what the king ordered should be done with these subjects who rejected him—they were to be brought before him and **killed** in front of him!

If the destiny of people who reject Christ is eternal existence being tormented in the lake of fire, then Jesus would've certainly reflected it in this parable because the secondary purpose of this tale is to reveal the eternal fate of those who reject the Lordship of Christ. Surely Jesus, the Son of God, could've easily come up with a clear way to reflect the doctrine of eternal torture in this parable (as well as his other parables). He could've said something like: "But those enemies of mine who did not want me to be king over them—bring them here and torture them in front of me, but be sure not to kill them, just torment them day and night, week after week, month after month, year after year, decade after decade. And all

---

[6] Also known as The Judgment of Living Nations or The Sheep and Goat Judgment.

the while I'll just kick back and pay no mind to it." Yes, I realize how ridiculous this sounds, but I want to illustrate how absurd and unbiblical this doctrine is.

Let's face it if a king or ruler were to do this in the real world, no one in their right mind would hesitate to declare him (or her) unjust, wicked and perverse, no matter how evil the subjects might be. By contrast, there's nothing wrong with a king or ruler justly, but mercifully, executing such wicked rebels.

Summing up, let me emphasize that Jesus taught this parable in part to back-up and reveal the scriptural truth of what will happen to those who reject him as Lord. What will happen to them? According to Jesus in this parable, they will be brought before the King of Kings and **killed** in front of him. This will be accomplished by simply casting them into the lake of fire where **raging fire will consume them** (Hebrews 10:26-27). Could Jesus be any clearer? His words coincide with the numerous passages we've already looked at.

" They Will Be Thrown into the Fiery Furnace"

Christ also likened the lake of fire to a "fiery furnace" in Matthew 13:42 and 50. Like Gehenna, "fiery furnace" is an excellent example of the lake of fire because it clearly indicates nothing other than incineration—total destruction of soul and body—as Jesus earlier declared in Matthew 10:28.

The Messiah most likely got this apt figure from the Old Testament Scriptures since he studied and preached from them. In the Old Testament "furnace" or "fiery furnace" is used in reference to complete incineration or refinement (e.g. Psalm 12:6), but never to undying conscious torment. For instance, after the obliteration of Sodom and Gomorrah, which is a biblical example of the second death (2 Peter 2:6), Genesis 19:28 says that there was only "dense smoke rising from the land, like smoke from a furnace."

Notice how the figure of "fiery furnace" is used in this Psalm:

> **At the time of your appearing**
> **you will make them** [God's enemies] **like a**
> **fiery furnace.**
> **In his wrath the LORD will swallow them up,**
> **and his fire will consume them.**
>
> **Psalm 21:9**

There's no mistaking here that "fiery furnace" refers to being utterly consumed by raging fire as God's enemies are shown to be **swallowed up and consumed by his fire** and *not* existing in a perpetual state of conscious roasting.

In Daniel 3 the fiery furnace was so hot that it killed Nebuchadnezzar's soldiers who simply went near it as they threw the three Hebrews into it (Daniel 3:22-23). The only reason Shadrach, Meshach and Abednego survived the fiery furnace was because of God's supernatural protection (verse 27).

"Furnace" was also used by the prophet Malachi in the last chapter of the last book of the Old Testament to describe the day when God will judge evildoers: "That day will burn like a furnace" and "not a root or branch will be left to them" for "they will be **ashes**" (Malachi 4:1-3). We will examine this passage in more detail shortly.

As you can see, "furnace" in the Old Testament consistently signifies complete incineration, destruction and death, but never perpetual conscious torment.

We can confidently conclude that, if God does not miraculously intervene, as he did with Daniel's three friends who were *not* harmed by the blazing furnace (Daniel 3:13-27), the ungodly who will be thrown into the fiery furnace of Gehenna will suffer the precise fate that the enemies of Shadrach, Meshach and Abednego hoped for them: **death by incineration** (Fudge 104-105).

Consuming Fire Will Consume the Enemies of God

This brings us to another proof text:

> **If we deliberately keep on sinning after we have received the knowledge of the truth, no sacrifice for sins is left, [27] but only a fearful expectation of judgment and of <u>raging fire that will consume the enemies of God</u>.**
>
> **Hebrews 10:26-27**

Notice clearly that raging fire will utterly consume God's enemies on Judgment Day, not sadistically torture them without end. The Greek word translated as 'consume' here literally means "to eat" and is translated as "devour" in the King James Version. We can soundly conclude that **raging fire will literally devour God's enemies** when they're cast into the lake of fire—consuming them wholly.

This brings to mind James 5:1-5, which issues a warning to rich oppressors. Verse 3 states: "Your gold and silver are corroded. Their corrosion will testify against you and **eat your flesh like fire**." The word "testify" indicates that James is referring to a time of judgment; this is made clearer in verse 5: "You have lived on earth in luxury and self-indulgence. You have fattened yourselves in the day of slaughter." "The day of slaughter" is, of course, a reference to "the day of judgment and destruction of ungodly men" (2 Peter 3:7). Notice that the Day of Judgment is referred to as "the day of *slaughter*" and not "the day of the beginning of everlasting conscious torment" (sounds absurd, doesn't it?). That's because the Day of Judgment is a day of slaughter where the sins of God's enemies will testify against them and "eat their flesh like fire"— raging fire will utterly consume them just as declared in Hebrews 10:27 above.

It is fitting, incidentally, that James refers to the Day of Judgment as the day of slaughter since Gehenna, the biblical example of the lake of fire and often translated as "hell," was otherwise known as "the Valley of Slaughter" (see Jeremiah 7:30-34 and 19:2-13).

Examples of God Consuming His Enemies throughout History

The New Testament declaration that God will ultimately destroy his human enemies—soul and body—by raging, consuming fire is in perfect harmony with the many historical cases of how God dealt with his enemies in the Old Testament. Here's one example:

> **Aaron's sons Nadab and Abihu took their censors, put fire in them and added incense; and they offered unauthorized fire before the LORD, contrary to his command. [2] So <u>fire came out from the presence of the LORD and consumed them, and they died before the LORD</u>.**
> **Leviticus 10:1-2**

Nadab and Abihu ignored God's commands and attempted to approach Him on their own terms so "fire came out from the presence of the LORD and **consumed them**, and they **died** before the LORD." Their disregard for the LORD's will and attempt to approach Him on their own terms represents religion as opposed to Christianity. Religion is the human attempt to connect with God whereas Christianity is God connecting with humanity through Christ. We can either do it our way or God's way; it's our choice.

The fiery consumption of Nadab and Abihu is a biblical *example* of what will happen on Judgment Day to people who disregard God's Word and live their lives with little or no concern of their Creator; such proud rebels are only willing to approach God on their own terms. On Judgment Day these fools can expect a fire to come out from the presence of the LORD and consume them. They will die before the LORD just as assuredly as Nadab and Abihu did.

Here are some more examples:

And fire came out from the LORD and consumed the 210 men [Korah's followers] **who were offering the incense.**

Numbers 16:35

Elijah answered the captain, "If I am a man of God, may fire come down from heaven and consume you and your fifty men!" Then fire fell from heaven and consumed the captain and his men.[7]

2 Kings 1:10

...righteousness and justice are the foundation of his throne.
3 Fire goes before him
and consumes his foes on every side.

Psalm 97:2-3

Fire blazed among their [Dathan's] **followers;**
a flame consumed the wicked.

Psalm 106:18

"So I will pour out my wrath on them [the sinful people of Judah] **and consume them with my fiery anger, bringing down on their own heads all they have done, declares the Sovereign LORD."**

Ezekiel 22:31

Just as God dealt with his enemies in the past, so he will deal with his adversaries in the future at the Second Coming of Christ when God's consuming fire will strike the whole earth and "Babylon":

Neither their silver nor their gold
will be able to save them
on the day of the LORD's wrath.
In the fire of his jealousy

---

[7] This exact same judgment came upon another captain and his fifty men, as detailed in verse 12.

> the whole world will be consumed
> for he will make a sudden end
> of all who live on the earth.
>
> **Zephaniah 1:18**

Therefore in one day her plagues will overtake her ["Babylon"]:
   death, mourning and famine.
She will be consumed by fire,
   for mighty is the Lord God who judges her.
⁹ When the kings of the earth who committed adultery with her and shared her luxury see the smoke of her burning, they will weep and mourn over her.

Revelation 18:8-9

As you can plainly see, the fact that the LORD is going to destroy his human enemies by consuming fire at the second death perfectly coincides with how God has dealt with his human enemies throughout history. This is testimony to the unchanging, consistent character of God (see Psalm 102:26-27, James 1:17 and Hebrews 13:8). Wouldn't it be strange and totally inconsistent with God's just, merciful character as revealed throughout history if he sentenced his human enemies to never-ending roasting torment on Judgment Day—a sadistic, unjust, merciless sentence diametrically opposed to his consistent, unchanging character? Of course it would.

Notice in all the above passages that God does not wickedly torture these people with fire. No, **the fire consumes them.** No doubt there's an amount of terror and conscious pain to this type of execution, but it's not sadistically never-ending; it mercifully results in death.

Is this unjust on God's part? Not at all. Notice Psalm 97:2-3 above: Before stating that God will judge and destroy his enemies with consuming fire, it assuredly states that "righteousness and justice are the foundation of his throne." You see, we can always be confident of the fact that the LORD's judgments are completely righteous and just; and God is not quick in making a judgment. He is "compassionate and gracious, slow to anger abounding in love" (Psalm 103:8); "He is patient… not wanting anyone to **perish**, but everyone to come to **repentance**" (2 Peter 3:9). Yet, there's a limit to God's patience and mercy if a stubborn person continually chooses to resist and rebel against Him; and when his patience and mercy end, his judgment begins. Yet even God's judgments are balanced by his mercy and justice.

" They Will Be Ashes under the Soles of Your Feet"

The very last chapter of the Old Testament also reveals how God's enemies will be utterly consumed in a fiery "furnace:"

> "Surely the day is coming; it will <u>burn like a furnace</u>. All the arrogant and every evildoer will be stubble, and that day that is coming <u>will set them on fire</u>," says the LORD Almighty. "<u>Not a root or branch will be left to them</u>. [2] But for you who revere my name, the sun of righteousness will arise with healing in its wings. And you will go out and leap like calves released from the stall. [3] Then you will trample down the wicked; <u>they will be ashes under the soles of your feet</u> on the day when I do these things," says the LORD Almighty…
> [5] "See, I will send you the prophet Elijah before the great and dreadful day of the LORD comes."
> **Malachi 4:1-3,5**

So ends the Old Testament, followed by a period of 400-years of silence between the testaments where God would not speak through Scripture prophecy. Like the final chapters of Revelation (the last book of the New Testament) the final chapter of Malachi (the last book of the Old Testament) contrasts the final destinies of both the righteous and the unrighteous: For those who revere God's name, "the sun of righteousness will arise with healing in its wings." They will experience warmth and healing in the light of the LORD's presence as God binds up their bruises, heals their wounds and wipes away every tear (see Isaiah 30:26 and Revelation 21:4).

The righteous will "go out and leap like calves released from the stall." In other words, just as a calf leaps for sheer joy when finally turned loose into the sunlight after being confined to a stall for extended periods of time, so it will be with those who revere God's name.

As for those who do not revere God's name, "all the arrogant" and "every evildoer," they will be *like* **stubble set on fire**; they will be burned up so completely that "**not a root or branch will be left to them**"; they will be **like ashes** under the soles of the feet of the righteous. These easy-to-understand figures eliminate any possibility of remnant or survivor. As Edward Fudge put it, a clearer example of literal destruction could hardly be given.

Thus ends the Old Testament with the righteous ultimately rejoicing in God's salvation and eternal life while evildoers are utterly destroyed—gone forever with no remnant or possibility of restoration.

Once again, there is no mention of people existing forever in a perpetual state of fiery conscious torment. All we see is a clear picture of "every evildoer" being utterly destroyed by raging, consuming fire.

Is Malachi 4:1-5 Applicable to Everlasting Destruction?

The above passage is such a stumbling block to the view of eternal torment that its advocates try to dismiss it altogether. They suggest that the text is referring to the battle of Armageddon on the day of Christ's Second Advent and is therefore not applicable to the second death.

So let's look at the scriptural facts and draw a sound conclusion:

The passage is referring to "the day of the Lord" (verses 1, 3 and 5). What is "the day of the LORD"? This phrase appears 19 times in the Old Testament and 4 times in the New Testament to express the time of God's extreme judgment and wrath.

These 23 passages do not all refer to the same specific judgment. For instance, in Ezekiel 30:3 "the day of the LORD" refers to a near future (now historical) judgment of Egypt; in Zechariah 14:1 and 2 Thessalonians 2:2 it refers to a far future judgment.

Two "day of the LORD" expressions yet remain to be fulfilled: **1.** At the end of the 7-year Tribulation period or Daniel's 70th week (see Joel 3:14), and **2.** At the end of the Millennium (see 2 Peter 3:10). Both of these specific judgments result in condemned people being thrown into the lake of fire: The Pre-Millennial Judgment of Christ will take place at the end of the 7-year Tribulation period (see Matthew 25:31-46) otherwise known as The Judgment of Living Nations; and The Great White Throne Judgment will take place at the end of the Millennium (see Revelation 20:11-15).

Malachi 4:1-5 is applicable to either of these judgments. This is in line with the prophetic "law of double reference," which simply means that prophecies often have two applications, typically a far flung one and a closer one.

Secondly, Malachi 4:1-5 coincides perfectly with a passage we've already examined, Matthew 13:40-43, which is an unquestionable reference to the second death. Observe how these texts parallel each other:

- **"Surely the day is coming; it will <u>burn like a furnace</u>."**
  Malachi 4:1a
- **"They** [the angels] **will throw them into <u>the fiery furnace</u>,"**
  Matthew 13:42

- "All the arrogant and every evildoer will be <u>stubble</u> and that day that is coming will <u>set them on fire</u>."

  Malachi 4:1b

- "As <u>weeds</u> are pulled up and <u>burned in the fire</u>, so it will be at the end of the age."

  Matthew 13:40

- "But for you who revere my name, <u>the sun of righteousness will arise</u> with healing in its wings."

  Malachi 4:2

- "Then <u>the righteous will shine like the sun</u> in the kingdom of their Father."

  Matthew 13:43

As you can see, both passages liken the lake of fire to a blazing furnace; both liken "evildoers" to combustible matter that will be burned up ("stubble" and "weeds"); both reveal that, after every evildoer is destroyed, the righteous will shine like the sun; and both show all that will be left of the ungodly will be ashes (Malachi 4 expressly states this in verse 3 whereas Matthew 13 implies it with the figure of "weeds… burned in the fire").

Since these are clearly coinciding passages both refer to the ultimate end of the ungodly in the lake of fire, the second death.

Thirdly, notice that Malachi 4:1 refers to a time when "*all* the arrogant and every evildoer" will be destroyed. Biblically, we know that *all* evildoers will not be destroyed until "the day of judgment and **destruction** of ungodly men" (2 Peter 3:7) when all "the wicked will be **no more**" (Psalm 37:10).

Fourthly, notice that Malachi 4:1 says that "Not a root or branch will be left to them" and verse 3 says that all evildoers will be "ashes." Both verses are figurative, but the picture they portray is clear: **There will be nothing left of the ungodly but ashes when God's raging fire consumes them.** They will be totally destroyed—both soul and body—as Jesus solemnly declared.

No mention is made anywhere of their souls living forever in a state of fiery conscious torment. If this perverse religious belief were true, why would the LORD leave out something of such importance? This is way too significant of a "detail" to leave out.

Lastly, it just makes good sense that the Old Testament would sign off with a clear declaration of the final destiny of both the righteous and the unrighteous just as the New Testament does.

In light of all this, we can confidently conclude that Malachi 4:1-5 is indeed applicable to human damnation.

The Example of the Death of Jesus Christ

The very death of Jesus Christ on the cross is an example of literal everlasting destruction. Jesus suffered God's wrath and died so that we don't have to. Theologians refer to this as "substitutionary death." All this means is that Christ suffered and died in our place; he was sacrificed for our sakes so that we don't have to reap the wages of our sin. As the Bible states:

> **...he suffered death, so that by the grace of God**
> **he might taste death for everyone.**
> **Hebrews 2:9b**

The Messiah suffered and tasted death for everyone. This is what God would have had to do to *us* on Judgment Day if Jesus hadn't suffered and died in our place. In other words, Christ suffered the very penalty that we were to suffer, and that penalty is **suffering that ends in death**.

Jesus didn't die for us so that we don't have to experience earthly death, the first death; he died for us so that we don't have to suffer the second death. **So Christ's death on the cross is a window for us of what the second death essentially is; and the only view we see through this window is suffering that ends in death, not never-ending conscious torture.** Unlike the ungodly people cast into the lake of fire, who will suffer everlasting destruction, Jesus rose from the dead "because it was impossible for death to keep its hold on him" (Acts 2:24b) (Fudge/Peterson 204). God had to raise Christ from the dead otherwise we would not be justified and have the hope of eternal life (see 1 Corinthians 15:12-22 and Romans 10: 9-10).

The bottom line is that Jesus "tasted **death** for everyone," he didn't taste eternal roasting torture for us, he tasted **death**. If Christ' substitutionary death had to consist of what supporters of eternal torture say the wages of sin is then Jesus would have to *still* be suffering never-ending torment. Are you with me?

Jesus' suffering and death in our place on this earth is a picture of what the second death will be on Judgment Day in the spiritual realm. And the simple fact is that Christ suffered and died; this is what people witnessed when he was horribly crucified and this is what we see today when we picture it. Death is what we are saved from not eternal torture, for "the wages of sin is death."

The Ungodly Will Lose Their Life—Soul & Body

Let's now observe how the Greek word, *apollumi,* is used in reference to unredeemed people ultimately **losing their very lives**:

> **Then he said to them all: "If anyone would come after me, he must deny himself and take up his cross daily and follow me. [24] For whoever wants to save his life will <u>lose</u> *(apollumi)* it, but whoever <u>loses</u> *(apollumi)* his life for me will save it. [25] What good is it for a man to gain the whole world, and yet <u>lose</u> *(apollumi)* or forfeit his <u>very self</u>."**
>
> **Luke 9:23-25**

Jesus says in the latter half of verse 24 that "whoever loses his life for me will save it." What exactly does this mean? Well, when a person is "born again"—repenting of sin and confessing Christ as Lord (Acts 26:20 & Romans 10:9-10)—he or she miraculously becomes "a new creation; the old is gone, the new has come!" (2 Corinthians 5:17). The spiritual part of their being is born anew. That's why Paul proclaimed, "I have been crucified with Christ and I no longer live, but Christ lives in me" (Galatians 2:20). This is basically what Jesus meant by "losing your life for him." So the Lord was simply saying that anyone who is spiritually born-again and all that goes with that will save his/her life.

This is in contrast to the person who tries to save his (or her) own life. As Jesus declares in the first part of verse 24, such a person will **lose his life**! If you're a believer, you've been "bought" and saved by God at a great price—the sacrifice of his Son, Jesus Christ. You are therefore "not your own" (1 Corinthians 6:19-20). People who reject Christ' sacrifice are essentially trying to keep or save their lives. They know that if they truly acknowledge the Lordship of Christ, they'll have to give up living for their fleshly desires and start living for God. This means that they'll have to give up (repent of) sin, but some people don't want to do this because they love their sinful lifestyles and don't want anyone telling them what they morally can or cannot do (see John 3:19-20). They don't want Christianity, they want Selfianity or Fleshianity. (Obviously they don't realize that God wants Lordship over our lives and instructs us to do or not do certain things for our ultimate benefit, not to "deprive" us). As Jesus points out here, such people will end up **losing their lives**.

This fact is reinforced in verse 25: "What good is it for a man to gain the whole world, and yet **lose** *(apollumi)* or forfeit his **very self**." Notice how the word "gain" is used in contrast to "lose" and "forfeit." We can conclude therefore that lose and forfeit would be the opposite of gaining something. With this understanding, notice what Jesus said a person who tries to "save his own life" will lose or forfeit: **his very self**!

The Greek word translated as "self" here is *heautou (heh-ow-TOO),* which simply refers to a person's selfhood, that is, a person's **very being**. It is therefore translated variously as "himself," "herself," "myself," "yourself," "ourselves," etc. In the matching gospel accounts of this verse—Matthew 16:26 and Mark

8:36—the word "soul" is used instead of self. "Soul" in these passages is translated from the Greek word *psuche (soo-KAY)* which can also be translated "life" in proper contexts, as is the case with verse 24 where Jesus said, "whoever wants to save his life *(psuche)* will **lose it**."

The conclusion we draw from this information is this: A person who rejects giving up his/her life for Christ will end up losing their life, their soul, their very self.

This exact thought is expressed by Jesus in this verse:

> **"Whoever tries to keep his life will <u>lose</u> *(apollumi)* it, and whoever loses his life will preserve it."**
>
> **Luke 17:33**

How much clearer could the Lord be? The only people who will preserve their lives for eternal life are people who are willing to give up their lives for Christ (which, once again, means getting born-again and thus being "crucified with Christ"; then growing spiritually from there). People who refuse to do this will lose their lives.

Let's look at one last similar expression from Jesus:

> **"The man who loves his life will <u>lose</u> *(apollumi)* it, while the man who hates his life in this world will <u>keep it for eternal life</u>."**
>
> **John 12:25**

Jesus isn't saying that Christians can't enjoy living while in this world (on the contrary, 1 Peter 1:8 says that believers will be "filled with an inexpressible and glorious joy"), he's simply teaching in line with the biblical fact that true Christians are strangers in this world (Hebrews 11:13 & 1 Peter 1:1) who "are looking forward to a new heaven and new earth, the home of righteousness" (2 Peter 3:13).

The reason Christians are said to be strangers in this world and "hate" their lives on earth [8] is because the present condition of this world is not the way God wants it to be. Consider, for example, the pain, death, disease, injustice, poverty, atrocities, immorality, wars and crime evident all over the earth.

All these evils are evidence that the devil is "the god of this world"; in other words, the whole world is under his influence or control (see 2 Corinthians 4:4 and 1 John 5:19). Revelation 21:1-4, on the other hand, reveals how our good, just, loving Creator wants life to be on earth: When he creates a "new earth" there will be "no more death or mourning or crying or pain, for the old order of things has passed away" (verse 4).

Getting back to the passage, Jesus is simply saying that a person who hates his or her life in this world in the above manner "will **keep it for eternal life**." By contrast, those who love their sinful, rebellious lifestyles in this wicked world and reject giving up their lives to Christ's Lordship will ultimately **lose their lives**.

When exactly will these selfish people who reject God's grace lose their lives, their souls, their very selves? Obviously on "the day of judgment and destruction of ungodly men" (2 Peter 3:7) where God will "destroy both soul and body in hell *(Gehenna)"* (Matthew 10:28).

In all these passages Jesus repeatedly stresses that ungodly people will **lose their very lives** if they don't accept the gospel. He says absolutely nothing about people keeping their lives and spending them in never-ending roasting agony in "eternal separation from God." This shows that this perverse belief is a false, unbiblical doctrine, which needs to be exposed for what it is. That's what *HELL KNOW* is all about.

---

[8] "Hate" here is translated from a Greek word which by extension means "to love less than" (Strong 48).

Examples of Literal Destruction—Not Eternal Torment

Let's briefly review the many **examples** of literal everlasting destruction that we've covered. Observe how the eternal torture position doesn't fit *any* of these:

1. The very word "hell" itself is an unmistakable example of literal everlasting destruction as *Gehenna,* the biblical word translated as "hell" in reference to the lake of fire, was a very certain **symbol of destruction** which all of Jesus' listeners readily understood.
2. Jesus and John the Baptist proclaimed that "at the end of the age" (i.e. Judgment Day) the unrighteous will be like weeds, trees, branches and chaff thrown into fire. It goes without saying that combustible articles like these **burn up in fire**. We also viewed similar examples from the Old Testament and the book of Hebrews.
3. In The Parable of the Ten Minas Jesus used the example of a king having his enemies **brought before him and executed** (Luke 19:27).
4. Jesus twice spoke of the lake of fire as a **"fiery furnace"**—an unmistakable figure of complete incineration as revealed in the Old Testament. Articles thrown into a furnace are **burned up,** not perpetually preserved.
5. We viewed many examples of how God consumed his human enemies by fire throughout history and saw that these examples perfectly coincide with the clear passages which state that God's enemies will be **consumed by raging fire at the second death** (e.g. Hebrews 10:27 and Psalm 20:9).
6. At the very end of the Old Testament we viewed an unmistakable example of ungodly people being likened to stubble set ablaze; **"not a root or branch will be left to them"** as they will be "**ashes** under the soles of [the righteous'] feet."
7. We discovered that the very crucifixion of Jesus Christ is an example of the second death. **Jesus suffered God's wrath and died on the cross**. He was sacrificed in our place. This is

a window for us to view the nature of the second death, and the picture we see through this window is that of **suffering that ends in death**, not never-ending fiery torture.

8. Lastly, we witnessed how these many clear examples are backed up by Jesus' declarations that those who reject God's sacrifice for their sins and try to "save their own lives" will end up **losing their lives, their souls, their very selves**.

As you can see from all these illustrations, not only does the Bible repeatedly declare that people will be destroyed in the lake of fire, as shown earlier, it also backs up these plain declarations with numerous easy-to-understand **examples of literal destruction**.

3

FURTHER PROOF
of Everlasting Destruction

Let's observe what the book of 2 Peter has to say about human damnation starting with a verse touched on earlier:

> **if he** [God] **condemned the cities of Sodom and Gomorrah by <u>burning them to ashes</u> and made them an <u>*example*</u> of <u>what is going to happen to the ungodly</u>...**
>
> **2 Peter 2:6**

The LORD tells us here precisely what the eternal fate of ungodly people will be: The utter destruction of Sodom and Gomorrah is His *example* of what will ultimately happen to them. How exactly did God destroy these cities? Why, by **burning them to ashes**.

We know this passage is referring to the second death because it says that ungodly people will experience a judgment similar to the incineration of Sodom and Gomorrah and the only time *all the ungodly* will experience such a fate is at the time of the second death where God will "destroy both soul and body" in the lake of fire (Matthew 10:28).

Jude also speaks of this example:

Even as Sodom and Gomorrah, and the cities about them in like manner, giving themselves over to fornication, and going after strange flesh, are set forth for _an example,_ suffering the vengeance of eternal fire.

Jude 1:7 (KJV)

As you can see, the Bible clearly says that Sodom and Gomorrah were destroyed by "eternal fire." Yet, how could this be since the fiery destruction of these cities took place 4000 years ago? This shows that the phrase "eternal fire" refers to **fiery destruction that lasts forever** when applied to human beings and not to eternal torture since the fire that destroyed Sodom and Gomorrah has long since gone out, but their destruction remains. As always, the Bible is clear if we simply allow it to interpret itself and resist the temptation to attach our own biased meanings to words and phrases.

Continuing with the book of 2 Peter, 3:7 says, "By the same word the present heavens and earth are reserved for fire, being kept for **the day of judgment and destruction of ungodly men**." Verse 9 continues, "The Lord is not slow in keeping his promise,[9] as some understand slowness. He is patient with you, **not wanting anyone to perish**, but everyone to come to repentance."

We addressed verses 7 & 9 earlier, but here's my point:

- 2:6 says that the ungodly will be **burned "to ashes,"**
- 3:7 that they will suffer "**destruction,**"
- And 3:9 that they will "**perish.**"

Peter, who walked with Jesus Christ throughout his 3-year earthly ministry, keeps bringing up the issue of the second death, yet speaks of it only in terms of incineration, destruction and perishing. He doesn't say anything at all about suffering perpetually in varying degrees of conscious torture. If this perverse belief were true, wouldn't this section of Scripture mention it

---

[9] The promise of a new heavens and new earth—see verse 13.

somewhere since it's specifically dealing with the subject of the second death, the eternal fate of ungodly people? I think being tormented forever and ever is much too important a detail to leave out, don't you? The obvious reason Peter didn't mention it is because this sadistic teaching is not a biblical doctrine. It's a myth, a satanic lie (which will be proven in the next chapter) that has been perpetuated for centuries by the formidable force of religious tradition.

"<u>Born</u> Only to be <u>Caught</u> and <u>Destroyed</u>"

Let's look at one other enlightening passage from the book of 2 Peter. This text refers to ungodly people "who follow the corrupt desires of the sinful nature" (as shown in verse 10):

> **They are like brute beasts, creatures of instinct, <u>born</u> only to be <u>caught</u> and <u>destroyed</u>, and like beasts they too will perish.**
> **2 Peter 2:12b**

Peter is speaking by the inspiration of the Holy Spirit here and what he's saying is obvious: "**Born**" is referring to being born into this world; "**caught**" is referring to the soul being held in Hades, which takes place after physical decease, where it "awaits" resurrection[10]; and "**destroyed**" is referring to what will happen after the soul & body are resurrected whereupon the person is judged and cast into the lake of fire. For verification, Revelation 20:13 says that "death and Hades gave up the dead that were in

---

[10] Whether one regards the state of the soul in Hades as conscious or dead is not pertinent to the subject of eternal punishment, which is the subject of this book. This is obvious because Hades concerns **the intermediate state of the soul between death and resurrection**. Since this is a *temporary condition* it is not relevant to our study on the eternal destiny of ungodly people. See *SHEOL KNOW* for more biblical information on the nature of Sheol/Hades or the article at the Fountain of Life site.

them" to be judged[11] and "If anyone's name was not found written in the book of life, he was thrown into the lake of fire" (verse 15).

What I want to emphasize is that 2 Peter 2:12 plainly teaches that ungodly people will be **destroyed in the lake of fire**, not preserved for roasting torture throughout all eternity. The Greek word translated as "destroyed" here is *phthora (fthor-AH)*. Paul used this very same word to describe our present mortal, "perishable" bodies in contrast to the immortal, imperishable bodies that believers will receive at their resurrection (1 Corinthians 15:42). This is yet another word that we can add to the seemingly endless list of biblical words that refer to the second death strictly in terms of destruction and perishment.

"Like Beasts They Too Will Perish"

Also notice in the above verse that ungodly people are likened to "brute beasts, creatures of instinct." The word 'beasts' here is translated from a Greek word which means "animals" (Strong 35). Now observe what the latter part of verse 12 says will happen to these 'animals': "and like beasts they too will **perish**." So the Bible likens unrighteous people here to animals, creatures of instinct, and emphasizes that they will ultimately perish in the same manner as animals. The question is naturally raised: How do animals perish? Do they perish by being consciously tortured forever and ever? Do they perish by having their "well-being ruined?" Do they perish by spending eternity "separated from God?" No, because none of these mean perishing. Animals perish simply by ceasing to exist (though, of course, some amount of suffering is involved in their perishing).

This is not an isolated instance in Scripture. Psalm 49:20 says that "A man who has riches without understanding is like the beasts that perish." The word 'beasts' in this verse likewise refers to

---

[11] *Hades (HAY-deez)* is the equivalent to the Hebrew *Sheol (sheh-OHL)* as a comparison of Acts 2:27 and Psalm 16:10 will verify; the former quotes the latter, supplanting the Hebrew *Sheol* with the Greek *Hades*.

"animals" (Strong 19). One might suggest that this passage is referring to the first death and not to the second death, but this can't be so because rich men *with* understanding as well as rich men *without* understanding will both ultimately suffer the first death. Besides, the writer says in verse 15 that "God will redeem my life from **the grave** *(Sheol);* he will surely take me to him." The psalmist confidently believed that God would redeem him from Sheol/Hades, whereas we can confidently deduce that "the man who has riches without understanding" will be resurrected from Sheol/Hades on the Day of Judgment to be judged and cast into the lake of fire, where **like beasts he will perish**.

Everlasting Destruction is Not a Denial of Hell

It's important at this point to emphasize that the view of literal everlasting destruction does not in any way deny the existence of hell. Although this is obvious I'm compelled to bring it up because adherents of eternal torture often try to give this impression. Let me give an example: A popular fundamentalist heresy hunter[12] had one of his sermons aired on the radio to defend the doctrine of eternal torment in response to the view of everlasting destruction.

The title of his sermon was "Why I Believe in Hell." There are two problems with this title. The first is that it gives the impression that adherents of literal destruction don't believe in hell while supporters of eternal torture do, but this isn't even remotely true. Adherents of both everlasting destruction and eternal torture believe that hell, the lake of fire, exists and that ungodly people will be cast into it on Judgment Day. The issue of contention is the *nature* of punishment people will experience in the lake of fire. The Bible calls it "the second death" (Revelation 20:14-15). Does this second death consist of eternal roasting torment or literal

---

[12] Most such "heresy hunters" are not interested in biblical truth but rather in hunting down and discrediting anyone who deviates from *their* idea of proper Christian orthodoxy; in other words, truth is not the issue, but rather blind adherence to the established and accepted teachings of *their* religious tradition.

everlasting destruction? You see, the issue is not whether hell exists, but what happens there.

The obvious reason supporters of eternal torment resort to such tactics is because they don't want people to be exposed to the monumental scriptural support for everlasting destruction. After all, if they can malign adherents of literal destruction as "heretics who don't believe in hell," most Christians won't even consider the immense biblical support for everlasting destruction. In short, if they can keep people from studying destructionism they can keep them from believing it. They take this approach because they cannot disprove literal destruction scripturally; they therefore resort to *misrepresenting* it in order to keep people from considering it altogether.

Another common avoidance tactic they implement is to say that everlasting destruction is a cultic belief because a few cultic or borderline cultic organizations adhere to it in one form or another. Such an argument successfully diverts attention from the proof of Scripture, which is where any teaching ultimately stands or falls. In chapter 6 we'll see why this argument holds no water in the section *'Cults Teach Destructionism—It Doesn't Look Good'*.

The second problem with the sermon title "Why I Believe in Hell" is the vagueness of the word 'hell.' Although 'hell' usually conjures up ghastly medieval images of people suffering eternally in fire pits, the term means different things to different people. It can just as easily provoke cartoony images of *The Far Side* comic strip or, to people like me, biblical impressions of Gehenna, the Valley of Hinnom (see the first section in chapter 2). My point is that advocates of literal destruction could just as well title a sermon "Why I believe In Hell," but refer to ultimate extinction of the ungodly with no hope of resurrection.

The reason supporters of eternal torment like to use the word 'hell' is because **it's a good cover-up term for eternal torture**. What do I mean? When they speak of 'hell' they're *actually* referring to never-ending fiery torment in separation from God with no merciful pause to the roasting misery. This, of course, is way too heinous of a concept to spell out in this manner, so they simply use 'hell' as a code word to covertly refer to it. A much more honest and accurate title of this man's sermon would be "Why I Believe in Eternal Torture of the Damned." Why are supporters of eternal torment so reluctant to honestly and accurately spell out what they really believe in this manner? Why do they hide behind code words and other misleading terms or phrases, like "perish," "death" and "eternal separation from God"? Obvious answer: Because if they spell out what they really believe it would expose their belief as the sadistic sham it is.

The bottom line is that the view of everlasting destruction does not in any way, shape or form deny the reality of hell, the lake of fire; all it denies is the Catholic church's traditional teaching that people will suffer never-ending roasting torture there.

Suffering Meted Out as Divine Justice Requires

It's also important to emphasize that the view of everlasting destruction allows for all the conscious pain that divine justice might require for any sinner to suffer according to his or her personal degree of guilt. In other words, the second death does not necessarily occur in an instant, but conscious life will be extinguished as any suffering experienced mercifully ends in death—eternal death—death that lasts forever.

This is a biblical principle regarding God's judgment and justice. Consider, for instance, 'Babylon' in the book of Revelation, which will be judged and **destroyed**, but is given "as much torture and grief as the glory and luxury she gave herself" **while being destroyed**:

> "**for her** [Babylon's] **sins are piled up to heaven**
>   **and God has remembered her crimes.**
> [6] **Give back to her as she has given;**
>   **pay her back double for what she has done.**
>   **Mix her a double portion from her own cup.**

[7] Give her <u>as much torture and grief</u>
<u>as the glory and luxury she gave herself</u>."
Revelation 18:5-7

As you can see, according to God's just judgment, conscious suffering will be meted out to "Babylon" in direct relation to the sinful excesses in which she indulged. She will receive punishment "as she has given," and this will apparently be doubled. Doubling the payback is in keeping with God's character as this is how He judged his own nation of Israel (see, for example, Isaiah 40:2 and Jeremiah 16:18). Revelation 18 goes on to inform us of the "torments" Babylon will suffer (verses 10 & 15). Yet this suffering will end in complete destruction as Babylon will be "**consumed by fire**" (verse 8), just as this entire present earth will ultimately be destroyed in preparation for the new earth (2 Peter 3:10-11).

Consider it this way, if you jumped into a bonfire, would you not experience conscious suffering for a brief period before losing consciousness and ultimately burning to death? Of course you would. It's the same principle with the second death when God casts the condemned into the lake of fire; the difference being that the period of suffering will be meted out to each individual according to their degree of sinful guilt as divine justice dictates. The period of conscious suffering may last a split second, a few seconds, one minute, an hour, a day, a week, or longer. It all depends on whom we're talking about. Are we talking about the little old ungodly lady who lives down the street or Adolf Hitler? Hitler is responsible for the horrible suffering and deaths of millions upon millions of people. Perhaps God will determine that he deserves to experience the suffering and death of those millions before his ultimate extinction. We don't know, of course; I'm just speculating. It's up to the Supreme Judge to decide.

Understanding this helps explain a couple statements Jesus made. For instance:

> **"But I tell you that <u>it will be more bearable for Sodom</u> on the day of judgment than for you** [referring to the people of Capernaum]**."**
>
> **Matthew 11:24**

Adherents of eternal torment have used this verse to support the idea that there will be varying degrees of ceaseless torture—as if never-ending torment isn't bad enough (rolling my eyes). For example, in the case of Capernaum, eternal torturists argue that the people of this city will receive a harsher judgment and, consequently, a greater degree of perpetual roasting torment. Malarkey. The whole point Jesus is making in this section of Scripture (Matthew 11:20-24 & Luke 10:12-15) is that the unrepentant cities of Korazin, Bethsaida and Capernaum, where he preached and performed great miracles, are guilty of even greater sins than the infamous cities of Tyre, Sidon and Sodom. Because of this, Jesus says it's going to be "more bearable… on the day of judgment" for Sodom than for these unrepentant cities. Please note that Christ said it would be more bearable **on the Day of Judgment**, not more bearable for all eternity experiencing fiery conscious torment in the lake of fire. Jesus is simply pointing out that, on Judgment Day, the second death will be more bearable for the people of Sodom than for the people of Capernaum according to divine justice. Why? Because the people of Capernaum are guilty of a greater degree of sin. That's simple enough to understand, isn't it? We should just allow Scripture to say what it literally says and not feel compelled to add to it or take away (Revelation 22:18-19). In this case, adherents of eternal torment read way too much into Jesus' simple statement, no doubt because they're desperate for biblical support of their position.

Jesus also implied that God's enemies would experience varying degrees of conscious suffering at the second death when he said that corrupt religious teachers would "receive the greater condemnation" (NRSV) or "will be punished most severely" (Mark 12:40 & Luke 20:47). We've already determined from numerous passages that the unredeemed will suffer utter destruction of soul in body at the second death, but—obviously—

some will justly experience a severer degree of suffering when this destruction occurs.

This aspect of the second death is actually comforting if you reflect on it. It suggests that **everybody's going to get exactly what he or she justly deserves on Judgment Day**. Throughout human history evildoers have unfortunately "gotten away" with their wicked deeds—murderers, molesters, sadists, rapists, robbers, charlatans, oppressors, tyrants, slanderers, false testifiers, perverts, etc.; but we can take comfort in the fact that God's justice will ultimately prevail and every unrepentant soul will justly "get what's coming to him or her."

Paul Relayed " The Whole Will of God" and "Fully Proclaimed the Gospel"

At this time I'd like to point out an important statement made by the apostle Paul. Aside from Jesus Christ, Paul is by far the most important figure in the New Testament. Over half of the book of Acts, which is a biblical documentation of the early church, is devoted to Paul's exploits in ministry. About one third of the entire New Testament and nearly two thirds of the epistles were actually written by Paul under the inspiration of the Holy Spirit (2 Peter 3:15-16).[13]

With this understanding, consider a statement Paul made to a group of elders from Ephesus:

> **"Therefore, I declare to you today that <u>I am innocent of the blood of all men</u>. [27] For I have not hesitated to proclaim to you <u>the whole will of God</u>."**
>
> **Acts 20:26-27**

---

[13] This is assuming Paul was the writer of Hebrews. If not, he wrote about one quarter of the New Testament.

Paul declares here that he is innocent of the blood of all people because he faithfully proclaimed "the whole will of God" or, according to the King James Version, he declared "all the counsel of God." Paul backed this statement up in his letter to the Romans:

> **So from Jerusalem all the way around to Illyricum, I have <u>fully proclaimed the gospel of Christ</u>.**
>
> **Romans 15:19b**

Why was Paul "innocent of the blood of all men"? Simply because everywhere he went he fully proclaimed the gospel—the *whole* counsel of God. Paul didn't hide anything that the Lord revealed to him; he didn't hide any aspect of the gospel message. He shared it all. He was therefore innocent of "the blood" of all people.

My point is that if Paul fully proclaimed the whole counsel of God, as Scripture verifies, then he would have certainly mentioned *something somewhere* about unrepentant sinners suffering eternal conscious torment *if* this doctrine were true. After all, this is way too important of an issue to forget to mention, yet Paul says **absolutely nothing about eternal fiery torture anywhere** in his inspired writings or in his exploits as recorded in Acts.

Out of the fourteen biblical letters written by Paul (assuming he's the writer of Hebrews) in all but six of them he repeatedly made very clear statements about the eternal fate of those who reject the gospel of reconciliation. Although we've already looked at many of these passages, let's review them here. As you will see, viewing everything Paul consistently taught concerning the nature of the second death is illuminating and makes a powerful point.

Paul fully proclaimed the whole counsel of God by plainly declaring:

- That those who live a lifestyle of unrepentant sin "deserve **death**" – Romans 1:32
- That "all who sin apart from the law will also **perish** apart from the law" – Romans 2:12

- That sin "leads to **death**" – Romans 6:16
- That sin "results in **death**" – Romans 6:21
- That "the wages of sin is **death**" – Romans 6:23
- That those who live according to the sinful nature "will **die**" – Romans 8:13
- That the gospel is foolishness "to those who are **perishing**" – 1 Corinthians 1:18
- That "in Adam all **die**" – 1 Corinthians 15:22
- That those who preach the gospel are "the smell of **death**" "to those who are **perishing**" – 2 Corinthians 2:15-16
- That the Old Testament law "**kills**" and ultimately brings "**death**" – 2 Corinthians 3:6-7
- That the gospel is "veiled to those who are **perishing**" – 2 Corinthians 4:3
- That those who please the sinful nature "from that nature will reap **destruction**" – Galatians 6:8
- That "they will be **destroyed**" – Philippians 1:28
- That "their destiny is **destruction**" – Philippians 3:19
- That "they will be punished with everlasting **destruction**" – 2 Thessalonians 1:9
- That they "are **perishing**" – 2 Thessalonians 2:10
- That "they **perish** because they refused to love the truth and so be saved" – 2 Thessalonians 2:10
- That "Christ Jesus… has destroyed **death**" – 2 Timothy 1:10

We can add these next four *if* Paul was the writer of Hebrews:

- That they are like **worthless land** that will "in the end… **be burned**" – Hebrews 6:8
- That sins are "acts that lead to **death**" – Hebrews 9:14
- That raging fire "will **consume** the enemies of God" – Hebrews 10:27
- That those who "shrink back" in unbelief will be "**destroyed**" – Hebrews 10:39

In various ways with various words Paul was sure to repeatedly declare precisely what would happen to those who foolishly reject the gospel. He was sure to do this because God appointed him to fully proclaim the whole counsel of God. Paul didn't hide any aspect of the truth—including the awful truth that those who reject Christ will be utterly destroyed by the raging, consuming fire of the Lord. If words have any meaning at all then this is what we must conclude.

Moreover, if Jesus supposedly preached eternal torture, as many contend, then Paul would have certainly reinforced it. Yet Paul taught no such thing because Jesus taught no such thing, not to mention the Bible they taught from—what we know as the Old Testament—teaches no such thing.

Lastly, in Acts 20:26-27 (quoted above) Paul declared that he was "innocent **of the blood** of all men" because he didn't hesitate to share the whole counsel of God, including the unfortunate news of what will ultimately happen to those who reject the gospel. The very fact that Paul said he was innocent of *the blood* of all people shows that persons will actually die when they suffer the second death. Whether physical blood or spiritual blood, it doesn't matter: People's blood will spill on the Day of Judgment, which is called "the day of *slaughter"* in God's Word (James 5:5). Gehenna, often translated as "hell" in English Bibles and used as a symbolic reference to the lake of fire, was also known as "The Valley of *Slaughter."* "Slaughter" signifies that blood will be spilled, and the simple fact is this: **When blood is spilled people die**. Paul's statement makes no sense whatsoever if people don't really perish in the lake of fire. If people exist forever in conscious torment their blood would not be spilled at all—they'd still be alive, forever.

4

THE GREAT LIE:
The "Immortal Soul"

In light of the overwhelming scriptural evidence for everlasting destruction, how could anyone who knows how to read embrace the theory of eternal torment? What is it that prevents adherents of this position from accepting the monumental proof for destructionism literally? After all, don't they generally adhere to a literal view of the Bible?[14]

Actually there are a number of reasons why they refuse to take the Bible literally on human damnation, such as the influence of religious tradition, denominational allegiance and the corresponding sectarian bias, as well as job security and pride.

Perhaps the strongest reason is that they foundationally adhere to the doctrine of "the immortal soul," the teaching that every human being once created can never cease to exist (a less common name is "the eternal spirit"). Supporters of eternal torture cannot very well take such words as "die," "death," "destruction," "destroy"

---

[14] Interestingly, those who advocate eternal torture often refer to their doctrine as "the literal view," but it's not really a literal view at all because, as we've seen, they fail to take the Bible literally on human damnation. Everlasting destruction is the true literal view.

and "perish" literally if they believe that it's impossible for people to cease living.

Anytime you hear or read of "the immortal soul" spoken of as an unquestionable truth it indicates that the person speaking is an adherent of eternal torment. For instance, simply scan the Statement of Faith of various Christian organizations—whether it's for a church, denomination, magazine, college or website—and you'll quickly be able to ascertain if they embrace the doctrine of eternal torture. If they believe in "the immortal soul" they consequently *must* believe in eternal torture as well. If this is the case, their Statement of Faith will read something like this: "We believe in the immortality of the soul; that the righteous shall receive eternal life in communion with God and that the ungodly shall suffer eternal separation." Some may say "eternal punishment" rather than "eternal separation" but, regardless, what they really mean by these words is never-ending torment in the lake of fire. You see, because they believe human beings inherently possess undying souls they have no recourse but to conclude that every person will end up either living forever with God in eternal bliss or living apart from God in eternal torment.

The fact that the Bible continually warns that ungodly people will die, be destroyed, suffer death and be consumed by raging fire like weeds cast into fire is rendered completely irrelevant because of the doctrine of the immortal soul.

It is this belief in unconditional human immortality that propels the religious view of hell as eternal torture and prevents people from taking the Bible literally on the subject.

The "Immortal Soul" is Not Taught in the Bible

What's amazing is that the doctrine of the immortal soul cannot be found in Scripture. You can search in vain all you want, but you'll find no passage in the Bible saying that human beings possess immortality **apart from Christ**. That's because this belief did not originate from the Scriptures, but rather entered Judeo-Christian thought through contact with pagan Greek philosophy. The Bible teaches that God alone has immortality (1 Timothy 6:16) and he offers it to people only through the gospel: "... Christ Jesus, who has destroyed death and **has brought life and immortality to light through the gospel**" (2 Timothy 1:10).

The only support adherents of eternal torment can come up with for this immortal soul theory is to suggest that human beings are created "in the image of God" (Genesis 1:27) and therefore have an immortal soul and cannot die. Their reasoning is that God is immortal and therefore if human beings are created in His image then they must be immortal as well—that is, some core aspect of them, namely the soul (or mind or spirit), must be immortal. This argument assumes that being created "in the image of God" *must* refer to inheriting God's quality of immortality. The obvious problem with this line of reasoning is that God has other characteristics such as omnipotence (all-powerful), omniscience (all-knowing) and omnipresence (present everywhere at the same time), yet human beings have never possessed any of these characteristics even though we're created in the image of God.

Regardless, God did indeed bless the first man "Adam" [15] with the gift of eternal life when he created him. Adam *had* immortality.

There was, however, a *condition* to maintaining this immortality as God clearly instructed Adam that if he sinned he would "surely die":

> **And the LORD God commanded the man, "You are free to eat from any tree in the garden; [17] but you must not eat from the tree of the knowledge of good and evil, for when you eat of it <u>you will surely die</u>."**
>
> **Genesis 2:16-17**

---

[15] In the biblical Hebrew, *adam (aw-DAWM)* simply means "a human being (an individual or the species)" (Strong 8) or "the man" (see the NIV footnotes for Genesis 2:7 and 2:20).

The Hebrew word translated as "die" in this passage is *muwth (mooth)* which means "**to die**" or "**kill**" (Strong 63) and is repeatedly used in the Old Testament simply in reference to death, including the death of animals:

> **The fish in the Nile will <u>die</u>, and the river will stink;**
>
> **Exodus 7:18a**

> **They said to Moses, "Was it because there were no graves in Egypt that you brought us to the desert to <u>die</u>?"**
>
> **Exodus 14:11a**

If Adam never sinned he would've never died. Yet he did sin, and the instant that he did part of him died—his immortal nature. We know this because the aging process started that very day culminating in his death many years later (Genesis 5:5). God foretold Adam's death immediately after Adam's fall, "For dust you are and to dust you will return" (Genesis 3:19c). This helps us to understand why *muwth*—"die"—is actually used *twice* in Genesis 2:17. A more literal translation of this verse would read: "but you must not eat from the tree of the knowledge of good and evil, for when you eat of it, **dying, you will die**." In other words, the very day Adam sinned part of his being died, leading to his eventual demise.

The Hebrew word *muwth* always indicates that something has died or will die. It does not mean "separation" as some claim. If God meant to warn Adam that he would "separate" He would have used the Hebrew word *badal (baw-DAL)*. In Adam's case the death of his immortal nature was merely the consequence of a much deeper death—**spiritual death**. Spiritual death simply means that **the human spirit is dead to God**. If the human spirit is dead to God it is impossible to have a *relationship* with the Creator because the human spirit is the facet of human nature that "connects" with the LORD. As Jesus said: "**God is spirit**, and his worshipers must worship *in spirit* and in truth" (John 4:24). If a person is spiritually dead it is impossible to know and worship God in spirit and truth.

Why? Because they're spiritually dead to Him. Because they're spiritually dead to God they are separate from him, but 'dead' doesn't mean "separation"; rather separation from the LORD is the *result of* being spiritually dead to God.

This raises a question: What about Old Testament saints, like Moses and David, who were technically spiritually dead, but obviously had a relationship with the LORD? How was this possible? The answer is that they had a covenant with God, which is a relational contract. But their covenant was an *inferior* covenant because it failed to provide spiritual rebirth wherein the person literally becomes the temple of God in which the Holy Spirit lives *within* him or her (which isn't to say that the Holy Spirit didn't come upon certain individuals in the old covenant and anoint them, etc.). This is one of the main reasons the new covenant is referred to as a "superior" covenant (Hebrews 8:6) and, furthermore, explains what Jesus meant when he said that there was no one greater than John the Baptist, but the least person in the kingdom of God is greater than him (Matthew 11:11). How could *the least* in the kingdom of heaven—the Church—possibly be greater than John the Baptist? Because of spiritual rebirth and the fact that believers *are* the temple of God in the new covenant and not some structure as in the old covenant; that is, the Tabernacle and Temple.

The immediate spiritual death of Adam and Eve is evident by the fact that they hid from God and were afraid of Him (see Genesis 3:8-10). Their relationship with the LORD severely changed when they sinned as their pure communion died. Humanity has been hiding from God ever since. This is spiritual death—being dead to the Creator. Like Adam and Eve we've tried to cover up our sin with the fig leaves of religion, but religion can never solve the problem of spiritual death, including quasi-Christian religion. That's why Jesus, the second Adam, taught that we need to be spiritually regenerated to have a relationship with God (see John 3:3,6).

So the LORD originally created human beings with immortality, but it was *conditional* immortality. Unfortunately our primeval parents failed to live by this condition and consequently passed the curse of sin and death on to us all.

The Soul Can Die

For further biblical support that the human soul is not inherently immortal apart from redemption in Christ and can indeed die or be destroyed, let's go to "the creation text" which describes precisely how God created human beings:

> **And the LORD God formed the man from the dust of the ground and breathed into his nostrils the <u>breath of life</u>; and the man became <u>a living soul</u>.**
>
> **Genesis 2:7** (KJV/NIV)

The word "soul" in this verse is the Hebrew word *nephesh (neh-FESH)* which is equivalent to the Greek word *psuche (soo-KHAY)* used in the New Testament. [16] *Psuche* is of course where we get the words "psyche" and "psychology."

There has been a lot of theological debate concerning the exact definition of a human being. Yet, if nothing else, we can all agree that this verse reveals that human beings are living souls. At their core, human beings *are* living souls. Isn't this what the passage clearly says? God formed the human body from the basic chemical elements of the earth,[17] breathed into it the breath of life, and the man "became a **living soul**."

Because humans are essentially souls, the Bible often simply refers to people as such. For example: "All the **souls** *(nephesh)* that came

---

[16] When Old Testament passages are quoted in the New Testament, the Greek *psuche* is used for the Hebrew *nephesh*; for example, Acts 2:27, which quotes Psalm 16:10; and 1 Corinthians 15:45, which partially quotes Genesis 2:7.

[17] The notion that the human body is comprised of the basic chemical elements of the earth is a scientific fact not known until relatively recently, but our Creator revealed it here in Genesis 2:7 *thousands of years ago*.

with Jacob into Egypt" (Genesis 46:26 KJV). "Souls" in this verse simply refers to the *people* that accompanied Jacob to Egypt. Another example would be Joshua 10:28 where it shows Joshua taking the city of Makkedah and killing "all the **souls** *(nephesh)* that were therein" (KJV). In the New Testament Peter spoke of the "eight **souls** *(psuche)"* that were saved in Noah's ark (1 Peter 3:20 KJV); "souls" here obviously refers to the eight *people* that were saved in the ark. Most modern versions of the Bible would translate *nephesh* and *psuche* in the above three passages as "persons," "everyone" or "people" (see, for example, the New International Version).

In light of this biblical information it's obvious that "soul" *(nephesh/psuche)* in **its broadest sense** refers to *the whole person*, the whole human being—spirit, mind and body. In a **narrower sense** these Hebrew and Greek words for "soul" can refer to various facets of human nature. For instance *nephesh* specifically refers to a "dead body" in Leviticus 21:11 and Numbers 19:11; in Acts 14:2 *psuche* refers to the "mind"; and in Revelation 20:4 *psuche* refers to disembodied saints and thus to the entire immaterial facet of human nature—mind and spirit. (See Appendix B of the unabridged version of *HELL KNOW* for a more detailed study on the soul and human nature: spirit, mind and body).

Notice, incidentally, that the creation text also speaks of the "life" that God breathed into Adam. "Life" is translated from the Hebrew word *chay (KHAH-ee)* and is equivalent to the Greek *zoe (zo-AY)*, which is used in the phrase "eternal life" throughout the New Testament.[18]

The kind of "life" *(zoe)* that God originally breathed into Adam was eternal life; but, as we've already seen, this God-given gift of eternal life was *conditional*. Adam sinned and therefore failed to live by this condition; consequently, he lost the gift of eternal life. It's obvious that he still had life *(zoe)* after he sinned, as evidenced

---

[18] See, for example, 1 Peter 3:10, which quotes Psalm 34:12, or Acts 2:28, which quotes Psalm 16:11, both cases in which the Greek *zoe* supplants the Hebrew *chay*.

by the fact that he lived to be 930 years old, he just no longer had *eternal* life *(zoe)*. All of Adam's descendants—that is, everyone born into this world since Adam—**have inherited Adam's life *(zoe)* because we've all been born in his likeness and image** (Genesis 5:3).[19]

Thus no one born into this world intrinsically possesses eternal life because we've been born of the perishable seed of Adam. The only life *(zoe)* that people born of the perishable seed of Adam possess is the *temporal* life *(zoe)* which God "gives all men" (Acts 17:25). To inherit *eternal* life *(zoe)* we must be **born again of the imperishable seed of Christ**, the second Adam. This is what the gospel of Christ is all about. As it is written:

> **For as in Adam all die, so <u>in Christ all will be made alive</u>.**
> **1 Corinthians 15:22**

> **For you have been born again, not of perishable seed, but of <u>imperishable</u>, through the living and enduring word of God.**
> **1 Peter 1:23**

This helps us to understand why Jesus said we must be "born again" to see the kingdom of God in John 3:3,6. Also, notice the two polar opposite fates cited in the first passage above: "in Adam all **die**" but "in Christ all will be **made alive**." Enough said.

It's interesting to note that the very same Hebrew word *nephesh,* translated as "soul" or "being" in the creation text, is used 29 times in the Old Testament in reference to animals, albeit most English translations do not render *nephesh* as "soul" when used in this manner. For instance: "let the water teem with living **creatures** *(nephesh)*" and "let the land produce living **creatures** *(nephesh)*" (Genesis 1:20,24). *Psuche,* the Greek equivalent to *nephesh,* is also

---

[19] The entire human race was in Adam's loins. He was thus humanity's moral, spiritual and physical fountainhead and representative. **When he sinned he did not act as an individual person but as an entire race.**

used in reference to animals in the New Testament (for example, Revelation 8:9 and 16:3). As a matter of fact, "breath of life" is also used in reference to animals (e.g. Genesis 1:30). The question is automatically raised: If both humans and animals are "souls" animated or sustained by a "breath of life" from the Almighty, what's the difference between humans and animals? The obvious difference is that human beings—unlike base, instinct-oriented animals—are created "in the image of God." We thus have the capacity to know and worship God because we possess a higher spiritual dimension to our nature. Animals, of course, do not have a spirit as such. The spiritual dimension of human beings is contrasted by the sinful nature ("flesh"), which is the human proclivity to rebel against God and do evil. Animals likewise do not have a sin nature; since they are instinctual creatures their actions are neither good nor evil.

The bottom line is this: **Nowhere does the Bible state that the human soul, once created, is immortal and can never die.** *Nephesh,* the Hebrew word for "soul," appears over 750 times in the Old Testament and *psuche,* the Greek word for "soul," appears over 100 times in the New Testament. These over 850 references should tell us all we need to know about the soul, yet none say anything about it being immortal by nature. If the immortal soul doctrine were true, why did God inspire hundreds of references to the soul without mentioning anything about it being inherently immortal? On the contrary, God plainly informed Adam, who was a "living soul," that he would "**surely die**" if he sinned (Genesis 2:17). He also pointed out in Ezekiel 18:4,20 that "the soul *(nephesh)* who sins... will **die**." And, of course, Jesus plainly declared that God would "**destroy** both soul *(psuche)* and body in hell" (Matthew 10:28). A usual knee-jerk, but hollow, response is to argue that these Scriptures "are taken out of context." I would like to use this same argument by pointing out that biblical references to the immortal soul are taken out of context, but I can't *because no such passages exist.*

Obviously this idea that an unredeemed human soul cannot die or be destroyed is alien to the God-breathed Scriptures.

The Great Lie and the Tree of Life

The Bible reveals where this immortal soul belief originated. Remember what God said to Adam and Eve would be the consequence of disobedience? He warned them that they would "surely die" (Genesis 2:17). You see, the LORD made it perfectly clear way back in the beginning that going the wrong way—the way of selfishness and rebellion—would lead to **death**. This is in harmony with the biblical fact that "the wages of sin is **death**" (Romans 6:23). Yet when satan, "the father of lies" (John 8:44), tempted Eve to sin in Genesis 3:4, he contradicted what God said by saying that she would *"not* surely die" if she sinned. **This is the very first lie recorded in the Bible.** The devil was saying in essence, "What God said is a lie, you will not surely die—you have an immortal soul." Unfortunately people have been believing this lie about the so-called immortal soul ever since; this false doctrine infiltrated Christianity early on and has become the "orthodox" view even though the Bible does not teach it, thus proving the power of religious tradition and sectarian allegiance. This long-lasting mass deception explains why I refer to the doctrine of the immortal soul as **The Great Lie**.

After the unfortunate fall of Adam and Eve, notice what the LORD says to Himself:

> **And the LORD God said, "The man has now become like one of us, knowing good and evil. He must not be allowed to reach out his hand and take also from the tree of life and eat, <u>and live forever</u>."**
>
> **Genesis 3:22**

God would not have said this if Adam *already* possessed an immortal soul (i.e. unconditional immortality). Secondly, this statement makes it clear that human beings *can* obtain unconditional immortality **if** they eat of the tree of life. The obvious reason God did not want Adam to eat of the tree of life is because he was unredeemed. If Adam ate of the tree of life in his unredeemed condition he would have attained unconditional immortality and thus would have condemned himself and his descendants to live forever in a fallen, ungodly state (like the devil and his angels, which we'll look at shortly). The LORD is just, righteous and merciful and didn't want such a horrible tragedy to befall humanity so he immediately banished Adam & Eve from the garden and was sure to guard the way to the tree of life (verses 23-24).

The LORD would have to redeem humankind before allowing us to eat "from the tree of life and live forever." That's what the gospel of Christ is all about. And this explains Jesus' statement in Revelation 2:7, "To him who overcomes I will give the right to eat from the tree of life, which is in the paradise of God." Notice clearly that only those who are born of God and overcome the world by faith (see 1 John 5:4) have the right to eat of the tree of life and live forever. That's because, as we've already seen, **eternal life and immortality are only available through the gospel** (2 Timothy 1:10). God wisely doesn't want sinful, unredeemed people to inherit unconditional immortality because then they'd have to live forever in a fallen state miserably separate from their Creator. In such a scenario they would indeed have the gift of immortality, but this "gift" would actually be a curse. After all, what good is living forever if you have to live it in utter misery separate from your Creator, the very Fountain of Life (Psalm 36:9)?

Resurrection unto Unconditional Immortality

Eating of the tree of life may simply refer to the resurrection of the dead unto eternal life. You see, Jesus spoke of two different kinds of resurrections:

> **"for a time is coming when all who are in their graves will hear His voice ²⁹ and come out—those who have done good will rise to <u>live</u>, and those who have done evil will rise to be <u>condemned</u>."**
>
> **John 5:28-29**

The two different kinds of resurrections are clear: the righteous (those in right-standing with God) will rise to **live** while the unrighteous (those not in right-standing with God) will rise to be judged and **condemned** *if* their names are not found in the book of life (Revelation 20:11-15). I add the "if" clause for reasons shared in chapter **8** of the unabridged version of *HELL KNOW*.

Notice clearly that only the righteous will "rise to live"—only the righteous will be granted "life and immortality" (2 Timothy 1:10). If only the righteous will rise to live, it naturally follows that the other group will rise to *not* live. That is, they will be judged and condemned to the second death, the lake of fire, where God will "destroy both soul and body." We've already searched the Scriptures to see how plainly evident this is.

According to 1 Corinthians 15:42-54, the righteous who "will rise to live" will receive an **imperishable, glorified, spiritual** body at the time of their resurrection. Verse 54 speaks of this: "When the perishable has been clothed with the **imperishable**, and the mortal with **immortality**, then the saying that is written will come true: 'Death has been swallowed up in victory.' " Incidentally, some adherents of eternal torment, apparently desperate for proof texts, will cite this passage to support their view that "every human being will have immortality" (Menzie 244), yet even a novice student of the Bible can see that the passage *exclusively refers to born-again believers* (for example, see verse 50, which plainly shows that the people addressed are to "inherit the kingdom of God").

As you can see, this resurrection to eternal life is a resurrection to unconditional immortality. Those who "will rise to live" will never die—for "death has been swallowed up in victory." Jesus made this clear:

> **"The people of <u>this age</u> marry and are given in marriage. ³⁵ But those who are considered worthy of taking part in <u>that age</u> and in the resurrection from the dead will neither marry nor be given in marriage, ³⁶ and <u>they can no</u>**

> **longer die; for they <u>are like the angels</u>. They are God's children, since they are children of the resurrection."**
>
> **Luke 20:34-36**

Firstly, notice that Jesus speaks of two ages here:

1. "this age"—the present age in which we're living.
2. "that age"—the age to come, which is an eternal age.

Only those "who are considered worthy of taking part... in the resurrection of the dead" will experience the age to come. "The resurrection from the dead" in this passage *only refers to* the resurrection unto eternal life, which takes place in at least three stages, including the Rapture and Christ's Second Coming to earth when he sets up his millennial reign (see 1 Thessalonians 4:13-17 and Revelation 20:4-6); it does not refer to the resurrection unto condemnation.

Secondly, notice what Jesus says about the righteous people who are worthy of partaking in this resurrection: He says that "they can **no longer die**; for they are *like* the angels." This shows that the resurrection of the righteous is a resurrection unto unconditional immortality. We who partake in this resurrection "can no longer die"; that is, no matter what, death—the cessation of life—will never be a possibility for us throughout eternity. This is supported by Revelation 20:6, which says that **the second death has no power over those who take part in this resurrection**. Since believers will be immortal and can never die, the second death has no power over them.

Thirdly, notice that Jesus says the righteous "can no longer die; for they are *like* the angels." Jesus doesn't say these righteous people would become angels, but rather that they would be *like angels* in the sense that they "can no longer die." This shows that angelic beings possess the God-given gift of intrinsic unconditional immortality. No matter what, angelic beings can never die—even if they choose to rebel against their Creator, like the devil and his loser demons, which we'll look at in the next section.

This resurrection unto eternal life and immortality is a fundamental aspect of the gospel of Christ. Acts 17:18 says that Paul preached "the good news about Jesus **and the resurrection**" and "for **his hope in the resurrection of the dead** he was put on trial" (Acts 23:6). Unfortunately you won't hear much emphasis on the resurrection of the dead unto eternal life in many churches today. It's more likely you'll hear about "going to heaven" when you die, as this belief seems to have supplanted the doctrine of the resurrection unto eternal life in importance. This was a byproduct of Augustine's false doctrine amillennialism, which is addressed in chapters **7** and **9** of the unabridged version of *HELL KNOW*. For a biblical look at the nature of eternal life see the corresponding articles at the Fountain of Life site.

' *What about the Devil and his Angels?* '

As noted above, Jesus said that angelic beings can never die; that is, they intrinsically possess unconditional immortality. Therefore even if some of them would choose to rebel against their Creator—like the devil and his angels (Isaiah 14:12-14)—they would *still* possess immortality and hence can never die. Why? Because their immortality is unconditional.

At the end of this age, what has God decided to ultimately do with the devil and his angels who have chosen to rebel against Him and who are obviously beyond redemption? The Bible teaches that the lake of fire is an "**eternal fire *prepared for* the devil and his angels**" (Matthew 25:41). This passage shows that God originally created the lake of fire as an eternal habitation for the fallen angels who chose to reject his Lordship. Revelation 20:10 reveals what will happen to the devil and his angels when they're cast into the lake of fire at the end of this age: "And the devil, who deceived them, was thrown into the lake of burning sulfur, where the beast and the false prophet had been thrown. They will be tormented day and night forever and ever."

As Christ plainly said in Matthew 25:41, *the lake of fire was not prepared for human beings*, but for the devil and his angels. Yes, God will use the lake of fire to execute "the second death" of human beings as we have clearly seen in this study, but **the lake of fire was not originally created for people**. Obviously the nature of the lake of fire is such that it will utterly extinguish any being that lacks immortality.

The devil and his angels, on the other hand, will not experience death in the lake of fire because they possess unconditional immortality; the very nature of Gehenna will torment them. This explains why **the lake of fire is never referred to as "the second death" in reference to the fallen angels, but only in regard to human beings** (e.g. Revelation 2:11, 20:6,14 & 21:8). Why? Obviously because people will be literally destroyed there, not preserved and endlessly tormented.

Adherents of eternal torture often cite the above verse, Revelation 20:10, to support their view by suggesting that "the beast and the false prophet" are human beings and this passage shows that they will be tormented day and night forever and ever. Their suggestion is that "the beast" refers to the antichrist and the false prophet is his prophetic cohort. Well, what does the rightly-divided Word of God teach on the matter? The antichrist is indeed a human being and is described in Scripture as "the *man* doomed to **destruction**" (2 Thessalonians 2:3). However, "the beast" from Revelation 19:20 and 20:10 is not referring to this man, but to the evil spirit that possessed him. This is clear because the Bible plainly says that **the beast originated from the Abyss** (Revelation 11:7 & 17:8). "The Abyss," according to Scripture, is the furnace-like pit **where evil spirits are imprisoned**, *not* human beings (see Luke 8:31, Revelation 9:1-2 and 20:1-3). I can therefore assure you that "the man doomed to destruction" from 2 Thessalonians 2:3 did not originate from the Abyss, but from his mother's womb! Likewise, the false prophet is referred to as *"another* beast" (13:11-17, 16:13 & 19:20). The Greek for "another" here is *allos (AL-los),* which means "another of the same kind." Therefore the "false prophet" is an evil spirit that originated from the Abyss as well.

For further proof that the beast and the false prophet are evil spirits and not human beings, consider Revelation 16:13: "Then I saw three evil spirits that looked like frogs; they came out of the mouth of the dragon [satan]; out of the mouth of the beast; and out of the mouth of the false prophet." Notice that the beast and the false prophet are spoken of on par with the devil himself; this signifies that they are **evil spirits of the highest ranking**, not human beings; in fact, they may be separate manifestations of satan.[20]

Secondly, notice that evil spirits come out of the mouth of the beast and false prophet just as they come out of the mouth of the devil.

Lastly, the Bible shows both the human antichrist and his human prophetic partner performing spectacular miracles, such as "causing fire to come down from heaven" (e.g. Revelation 13:1-18 and 19:20). For unbelievers to do this they would have to be possessed by high-ranking demons or satan himself, as no unredeemed human could perform such miracles. Such miraculous phenomena always stem from a supernatural source. In this case, the source of these miracles is the beast and the second beast that will possess the antichrist and his partner.

Some might argue that I'm admitting that God will allow some of his created beings to suffer everlasting torment. In light of this, why do I have a problem if this applies to human beings? Mainly because I understand what God's Word clearly teaches from Genesis to Revelation concerning the eternal fate of ungodly people, as revealed in this book.

Secondly, because I *am* a human being and consequently have firsthand knowledge of the human experience and condition. I therefore have the capacity to make sound judgments on human affairs based on the universal moral and judicial instincts that God has granted all people created in His likeness. And my judgment of

---

[20] If this is so, the dragon, the beast and the false prophet could be viewed as a sort of "unholy trinity," a blasphemous perversion of the Father, Son and Holy Spirit.

this doctrine of never-ending torture of human beings is that it is a heinous, revolting, perverse teaching—completely blasphemous to the just, moral, loving, merciful name of the Great I AM (God).

Thirdly, because I'm not an angelic being, have no comprehension of the nature of their existence in the spiritual realm, and only know about these entities by faith through a smattering of non-detailed passages in the Scriptures; I therefore have no recourse but to trust that God's eternal judgment of the fallen angels is just and righteous.

Lastly, because the devil is directly responsible for the fall of humankind and, hence, all the horrible evil and suffering that's ever been experienced on earth throughout history, I'm therefore not overly disturbed by the idea that he & his filthy minions have to suffer forever in a state of torment. The thought of any being suffering such a fate is tragic, but I think that the devil and his angels—who, unlike humans, have existed for millennia—were quite aware of the consequences of their foolish rebellion against the Almighty. As such, I can't help but feel they perhaps deserve their fate.[21]

Remember Jesus' statement from Luke 20:35-36 that, when the righteous are resurrected, they "can never die; for they are *like the angels"?* The righteous will become *like* the angels in the sense that they will inherit unconditional immortality and thus will never again be able to die. The righteous will, in essence, become "immortal souls." This is the only sense that the immortal soul doctrine is biblically valid. The downside to this is that if any partakers of this resurrection should choose to rebel against God at

---

[21] The Bible says the devil "prowls around *like* a roaring lion looking for someone to devour" (1 Peter 5:8), but he's a counterfeit "lion" whereas Jesus Christ is the genuine Lion of Judah. You could say that satan is a clawless, toothless, sinew-less, CLUELESS "lion." He's so *clueless* that he thought he could succeed in his original rebellion, which got him and his loser followers cast out of heaven (Luke 10:18). He's so *clueless* that he's going to deceive the nations for a doomed rebellion against the Lord in Jerusalem at the end of the Millennium, which God will easily dispel with fire from heaven (Revelation 20:7-10). *Talk about Clueless.*

some point in the age to come they would have to suffer the same fate as the devil and his angels. Why? Naturally because they possess unconditional immortality and can never die.

This shows that the Almighty's sentence of the devil & his loser demons to eternal torment in the lake of fire is *both* **punitive** and **exemplary**. Let me explain: Since these fallen angels possess unconditional immortality and *cannot* die the LORD created the lake of fire as their eternal prison, which is their **eternal judgment & punishment**. This, *in turn*, will serve as **an example** to all His creatures in the eternal age-to-come, including human beings. I seriously doubt that any of us will rebel in the age-to-come in light of the everlasting example of the devil & his foolish followers, but the possibility will exist since people will always possess free moral agency. After all, God would take little joy in creating robots *programmed* to love and obey him.

I should point out that there are many adherents of everlasting destruction who reject this idea that fallen angels will suffer never-ending torment in the lake of fire. They believe that they too will ultimately cease to exist, even if it takes eons of time. I have open-mindedly considered their position, but am persuaded by Scripture in maintaining the stance presented here. However, this is a detail matter and shouldn't cause division. Who cares about the devil & his loser demons anyway? I don't.

God's Gift of Eternal Life is the Answer to Humanity's Quest for Immortality and ' the Fountain of Youth'

Think about it, what is humanity's greatest desire—a greater desire than wealth, fame, true love or sexual gratification? From the ancient epic of *Gilgamesh* to Ponce De Leon's obsessive search for the fountain of youth to our modern-day compulsion to be youthful-looking as long as possible, humanity is obsessed with the idea of immortality, the idea of living forever. Wise King Solomon reflected on this compulsion:

> **I have seen the burden God has laid on men.**
> **[11]He has made everything beautiful in its time.**
> <u>**He has also set eternity in the hearts of men**</u>**; yet**
> **they cannot fathom what God has done from**
> **beginning to end.**
> **Ecclesiastes 3:10-11**

Although everything in all creation, whether living or non-living, is beautiful in its prime—women, men, animals, trees, mountains, buildings—they all ultimately crumble into dust. Everything has its set time but ultimately dies or decays. The Bible refers to this as the creation's "bondage to decay" (Romans 8:21). Despite this, there's this yearning in our hearts to live forever, a yearning to never die, a yearning for immortality or "the fountain of youth." We instinctively *know* we were created for immortality, but our immortality was somehow lost. Our fore-parents, Adam and Eve, possessed immortality but lost it due to sin. We therefore have this natural emptiness inside of us, an intense yearning for that which was lost—immortality and communion with God.

This deep yearning is what prompted a young rich man to approach Christ and ask: "Teacher, what good thing must I do to get eternal life?" (Matthew 19:16). The man was rich and had everything money could buy, but he lacked immortality. He knew he was inherently mortal and doomed to perish one day, despite his great wealth. And this explains why he asked Jesus how he could obtain eternal life. Christ answered, "If you want to **enter life**, obey the commandments" (verse 17). The Lord pointed the rich youth to the Old Testament law because the law is the schoolmaster that ultimately leads us to Christ through whom comes eternal life. Notice that Jesus didn't contest the man's question. He didn't say, "Young man, you *already* possess immortality and thus have eternal life." Jesus didn't say this because it's simply not true; instead he explained to him what he had to do to obtain eternal life.

On another occasion an expert in the law asked the Messiah a similar question: "What must I do to inherit eternal life?" (Luke 10:25). Like the rich man, the lawyer knew he was mortal and doomed to die one day. He didn't believe he had some "immortal soul." He thus asked Christ what he must do to inherit eternal life. And, once again, Jesus didn't contest the man's question. He didn't assure him that he inherently possessed immortality. No, like the rich man, the Lord pointed the lawyer to the Law and said, "Do this and you **will live**" (verse 28).

My point is that Christianity at its core is the answer to humanity's age-old quest for immortality. If you're searching for the "fountain of youth," the answer is revealed clearly in the Holy Scriptures, the revelation of Jesus Christ. Religionists may have obscured this truth over the centuries with their tangled web of life-stifling half-truths and lies, but the truth is still there, it cannot be quenched: **"The wages of sin is death, but the gift of God is eternal life in Christ Jesus our Lord"** (Romans 6:23).

Biblical Christianity is the true "fountain of youth" that humanity's been seeking since time immemorial.

5

BIBLICAL ANALYSIS
of Claimed Support Texts for Eternal Torment

Since the Bible doesn't teach that unredeemed people possess immortality or that they will suffer eternal torment in the lake of fire, the only way adherents of these beliefs can defend their position is by milking a small number of passages for details that the entire rest of the Bible refutes. This chapter is devoted to honestly examining these passages. Ironically, a close examination of these texts actually provides further support for literal everlasting destruction.

Daniel 12:2: "Shame and Everlasting Contempt"

Our first supposed proof text for eternal torture is this passage from Daniel:

> **Multitudes who sleep in the dust of the earth will awake: some to <u>everlasting life</u>, others to <u>shame and everlasting contempt</u>. [3] Those who are wise will shine like the brightness of the heavens, and those who lead many to righteousness, like the stars forever and ever.   Daniel 12:2-3**

This passage speaks of two resurrections—the resurrection of the righteous **to everlasting life**, and the resurrection of the unrighteous **to shame and everlasting contempt**. Please notice that *only the righteous will be resurrected to everlasting life.* "Life" here is the Hebrew word *chay* (the equivalent of the Greek *zoe*), which simply means "living thing" or the state of being "alive" (Vine 138). This is the very same Hebrew word used to describe the "breath of life" that God breathed into Adam to animate him (Genesis 2:7) and the "breath of life" of animals as well (Genesis 6:17 & 7:15,22). This "life" is spoken of in the Bible as the express opposite of death (Deuteronomy 30:19 & 32:39). My point is that there's nothing profound or mystical about the word "life" here. It simply refers to life, the state of being alive—the condition of existence. According to the above passage only one class of humanity—the righteous—will be resurrected unto everlasting life.

What about the class of humanity that is resurrected unto "shame and everlasting contempt?" One thing's for sure, we know they won't be resurrected for the purpose of being granted life since only the righteous will be resurrected for this purpose; the passage makes this clear. The resurrection of the unrighteous is a resurrection of shame because they are resurrected for **the express purpose of judgment and condemnation.**[22]

As Jesus declared:

> **"Do not be amazed at this, for a time is coming when all who are in their graves will hear his voice, [29] and come out—those who have done good will <u>rise to live</u>, and those who have done evil will rise <u>to be condemned</u>."**
>
> **John 5:28-29**

---

[22] What about the unrighteous who *would* repent and turn to the LORD *if* they had the opportunity? See the sections in chapter 8 of the unabridged version of *HELL KNOW: Post-Mortem Evangelization: Salvation after Death?, Inclusivism and Restrictivism* and *Speculation—A 'Simulation Test.'*

As in the passage from Daniel, Jesus stresses that **only the righteous will be resurrected to live**. "Those who have done evil" will be resurrected for the purpose of judgment and condemnation. Condemnation to what? Condemnation to the lake of fire where they will suffer "the second death" (Revelation 20:11-15), which consists of God destroying "both soul and body," as Jesus plainly declared in Matthew 10:28. Isaiah 41:11-12 explains that the ungodly will be "shamed and dishonored" in the sense that they "will **perish**," "be **as nothing**, and **non-existent**" (NASB). This is the ultimate shame—to have one's life judged so defiled and worthless that it must be blotted out of existence and memory.

What about the "contempt" that the unrighteous will suffer, which is said to be everlasting? The Hebrew for "contempt" is *deraown (day-raw-OHN)*. It's enlightening to view this Hebrew word in another Old Testament passage, which also pertains to the eternal fate of the unrighteous. Here *deraown* is translated as "loathsome:"

> **"As the new heavens and new earth that I make will endure before me," declares the LORD, "so will your name and descendants endure. ²³ From one new moon to another, all mankind will come and bow down before me," says the LORD. ²⁴"And they will go out and look upon the dead bodies of those who rebelled against me; their worm will not die, nor will their fire be quenched, and they will be <u>loathsome</u> (deraown) to all mankind."**
>
> **Isaiah 66:22-24**

According to this passage, what will be "loathsome to all mankind?" The **dead bodies** of those who rebelled against the LORD! Notice that these people are **dead**—all that remains of them are their **lifeless "carcasses"** (as the KJV states). Just as a grotesque, rotting corpse would be loathsome to you or me, so the proud and wicked people who dared to rebel against the Almighty will be loathed and abhorred by the LORD and the righteous.

We observe further reinforcement that these rebels are dead eight verses earlier:

> **For with fire and with his sword**
> > **the LORD will execute judgment upon all**
> > > **men,**
> > **and many will be those <u>slain</u> by the LORD.**
> > > > > > **Isaiah 66:16**

The verse speaks for itself: On Judgment Day there will be many "slain by the LORD." The ungodly will be slain, not kept alive and sadistically tormented forever. Their carcasses will be loathsome to all humanity blessed with everlasting life.

(We'll examine the phrase "their worm will not die, nor will their fire be quenched" in the forthcoming section on Mark 9:43-48).

Lastly, immediately after informing us of the two classes of resurrections, Daniel 12:3 denotes how the righteous will "shine like the brightness of the heavens... like the stars forever and ever." Notice that the passage fails to share anything about the state of existence of those who are resurrected "to shame and everlasting contempt." Why? Naturally because they'll be "slain by the LORD." In other words, since they *aren't* granted everlasting life, they'll have no existence of which to speak. They'll be *dead*—revolting carcasses, condemned to death for all eternity.

" There will be Weeping and Gnashing of Teeth"

Let's now examine a phrase Jesus used that adherents of eternal torture often cite to support their view:

> **"As the weeds are pulled up and burned in the fire, so it will be at the end of the age. [41] The Son of Man will send out his angels, and they will weed out of his kingdom everything that causes sin and all who do evil. [42] They will <u>throw them</u>**

> <u>into the fiery furnace, where there will be</u>
> <u>weeping and gnashing of teeth…</u>
> [49] **"This is how it will be at the end of the age.**
> **The angels will come and separate the wicked**
> **from the righteous** [50] **and <u>throw them into the</u>**
> <u>**fiery furnace where there will be weeping and**</u>
> <u>**gnashing of teeth.**</u>**"**
> Matthew 13:40-42, 49-50

The key phrase that eternal torturists use to support their position is, of course, "there will be weeping and gnashing of teeth." The Bible shows Jesus using this phrase four other times in Matthew (8:12, 22:13, 24:51 & 25:30) and once in Luke (13:28).

Devotees of never-ending misery claim that Jesus was saying, "They will endlessly weep and gnash their teeth in roasting torment forever and ever." But this is not what Jesus said. We need to be careful to let a biblical passage speak for itself and resist the temptation to read more into it based on our sectarian biases. When we read more into a simple statement like this we become guilty of *adding* to the Word of God, which is squarely condemned in Scripture (Proverbs 30:6, Revelation 22:18 & Deuteronomy 4:2, 12:32).

"Weeping and gnashing of teeth" is simply a solemn reminder that "It is a dreadful thing to fall into the hands of the living God" (Hebrews 10:31) for God's enemies will experience "a fearful expectation of judgment and of **raging fire that will consume the enemies of God**" (Hebrews 10:27).

Regarding the "weeping," if you were an unrepentant rebel against God, would you not be weeping the day you finally fell into His hands for judgment? And would you not be wailing as you are judged unworthy of living and subsequently cast into a vast fiery furnace? And would you not wail the entire time it takes the fire to consume you—however long that would justly be? Of course you would. That's why James warned rich oppressors to weep and wail for fear of God's coming judgment, referred to as "the day of **slaughter**," when fire will "**devour**" them (James 5:1-5).

As for "gnashing of teeth," most of us might think that this is a reference to the experience of pain, but Edward Fudge interestingly points out that "gnashing of teeth" in the Bible describes the wrath of an adversary about to kill his victim. In other words, the teeth belong to the tormentor, not the tormented (see Job 16:9, Psalm 35:16, 37:12, Lamentations 2:16 and Acts 7:54). Psalm 112 is the only exception. The psalm starts by stating "Blessed is the man who fears the LORD" and goes on to describe such a person in verses 2-9. The final verse mentions the wicked person by contrast:

> **The wicked man will see and be vexed,**
>   **he will gnash his teeth and <u>waste away</u>;**
>   **the longings of the wicked will come to**
>   **<u>nothing</u>.**
>   **Psalm 112:10**

As in the other passages that use the phrase "gnashing of teeth," the wicked man's gnashing of teeth is evidently an expression of fury against the righteous. Yet even while he grinds his teeth in ineffective rage, he **wastes away** and comes to **nothing**. The phrase could, in this one instance, be interpreted as a reference to pain, but the pain clearly does not last forever; the gnashing of teeth ends and the person is ultimately extinguished.

Edward Fudge's conclusion on "weeping and gnashing of teeth" is well expressed:

> *In scriptural usage the expression 'weeping and gnashing of teeth' seems to indicate two separate activities. The 'weeping' reflects the terror of the doomed as they begin to realize that God has rejected them and as they anticipate the execution of his sentence. 'Gnashing of teeth' seems to express their bitter rage and enmity toward God, who has sentenced them, and toward the redeemed, who will forever be blessed. The common assumption that 'weeping and gnashing of teeth' describes the everlasting agony of souls in conscious torment is the interpretation of a later age and lacks any clear biblical support (The Fire that Consumes, 104-105).*

Mr. Fudge does a fine job of wrapping up the matter, but let me add this: The reason I quoted the "weeping and gnashing of teeth" passage from Matthew chapter 13 above is because, unlike the other five times the phrase appears, Matthew 13 provides additional information to draw a sound conclusion. In verse 42 Jesus is still explaining The Parable of the Weeds, and therefore what he says must be interpreted in light of what he has already said. What did he already say? In verse 40 Christ says, "As the **weeds** are pulled up and **burned in the fire**, *so it will be* at the end of the age." Do weeds burn forever without ever quite burning up? No, they burn for a period of time until they **burn up**. It will be the same way with ungodly people on Judgment Day.

In addition to this, the Messiah describes the lake of fire in verses 42 and 50 as "the fiery furnace." As determined in chapter 2, "fiery furnace" is an unmistakable example of complete incineration. This is indisputable. By adding that "there will be weeping and gnashing of teeth" Jesus is simply describing the miserable way it will be on Judgment Day. Can you imagine the horrible scene it will be? The weeping, the wailing, the gnashing of teeth as God's enemies are cast into the lake of fire and **consumed by raging fire**? This is the only sound way we can interpret this phrase. After all, if Christ meant to say that these sinners would perpetually weep and gnash their teeth throughout all eternity, don't you think he would mention it somewhere? Yet he mentions no such thing. Instead he continually warned against the utter death and destruction of the second death, and backed it up with multiple easy-to-understand *examples.*

'What about "Outer Darkness" and "Blackest Darkness"?'

In three of the "weeping and gnashing of teeth" texts—Matthew 8:12, 22:13 and 25:30—Jesus refers to the lake of fire as "outer darkness" or, as the NIV puts it, "outside, into the darkness." Revelation 22:15 also refers to it as "outside." "Outer darkness" is merely one of many names the Bible uses for the lake of fire. Other names include Gehenna, burning sulfur, eternal fire and the second death. "Outer darkness" is a fit name for the lake of fire since it is the eternal spiritual realm prepared for the devil and his angels where the light of God's presence does not shine. When people are damned to "outer darkness" to suffer the second death, there will be weeping and gnashing of teeth, but God will ultimately utterly destroy both soul and body. That's why the lake of fire is referred to as "the second death" for unredeemed human beings, but not the devil & his loser angels who possess intrinsic immortality. The nature of the lake of fire is such that **it exterminates those who are mortal and torments those that are immortal**.

Jude spoke of wicked, godless people as "wandering stars, for whom **blackest darkness** has been reserved forever" (Jude 13). How do we harmonize this statement with the many passages that portray the lake of fire as a gigantic garbage dump where God's raging fire utterly consumes his human enemies? Obviously "blackest darkness" refers to the state of total oblivion. This is the blackest, most extreme darkness imaginable to the human mind—complete obliteration of conscious being in which there is no hope of resurrection or recovery. There is no blacker darkness than this. They "will be as nothing and non-existent" (Isaiah 41:12 NASB) or as Obadiah put it:

> ...they shall be as <u>though they had not been</u>.
> **Obadiah 1:16b** (KJV)

" They Will Go Away to Eternal Punishment"

Let's consider one of the most frequently cited passages used to support eternal torment:

> ⁴¹ " 'Depart from me, you who are cursed, into <u>the eternal fire prepared for the devil and his angels.'"</u>...
> ⁴⁶ "Then they will go away to <u>eternal punishment,</u> but the righteous to <u>eternal life.</u>"
> **Matthew 25:41, 46**

Once again, the passage plainly declares that **only the righteous will be granted eternal life**. "Eternal life" *(aionios zoe)* literally refers the perpetual life of the age to come. If only the righteous will be granted eternal life in the age to come, then the unrighteous will obviously not be granted eternal life in the age to come. The Bible is clear about this:

> **Whoever believes in the Son <u>has eternal life</u>, but whoever rejects the Son <u>will not see life</u>, for God's wrath remains on him.**
>
> **John 3:36**

So what does Christ say will be done with the unrighteous in Matthew 25:41 and 46 above? One thing's for certain, he says nothing about eternal life roasting in utter misery. What he does say is that they will be cast "into the eternal fire," which is the lake of fire (verse 41), and that this is their "eternal punishment" (verse 46). Please note that Jesus said "eternal punishment" and not "eternal punish*ing*." There's a difference.

The word "punishment" is translated from the Greek word *kolasis (KOL-as-is)* which refers to a "penal infliction" (Strong 43) and is therefore a judicial sentence. Christ does not say what the penal infliction will be in this passage, only that it will take place in the lake of fire ("the eternal fire") and that this infliction will last forever (that is, take place in the age to come, which lasts forever). Since Jesus doesn't specify here what exactly the penal sentence is, we must therefore turn to the rest of Scripture for answers. "Scripture interprets Scripture" is an interpretational rule.

And we know elsewhere in Scripture that Christ plainly said God would "**destroy** both soul and body" in the lake of fire (Matthew 10:28) and Paul taught that the ungodly would suffer "**everlasting destruction**" (2 Thessalonians 1:9). Add to this the numerous biblical *examples* of literal destruction covered in chapter 2 and it is clear that the eternal punishment or penal sentence that the unrighteous will be condemned to in the lake of fire is everlasting destruction of soul and body—destruction of the whole person which lasts forever—and not eternal punish*ing*.

Let's also consider the fact that the Bible uses the word "eternal" to describe the results of an act even when it is clear that the act itself is not of endless duration. For instance, Hebrews 9:12 speaks of the "eternal redemption" that Christ obtained for us; yet no one absurdly supposes that this redemption will be an endless process that goes on through all eternity "because by one sacrifice he has made perfect forever those who are being made holy" (Hebrews 10:14). Also, Hebrews 6:2 speaks of "eternal judgment," yet no one ludicrously claims that the work of judging goes on forever and ever without end. In the same way the act of punishment need not go on endlessly for the punishment to be eternal. Like eternal redemption and eternal judgment, eternal punishment is eternal in the sense that **its results are eternal**.

Some contend that Jesus was teaching eternal torment by describing the lake of fire as "the eternal fire." Yet this is simply a name for—and description of—the lake of fire which was **"prepared for** the devil and his angels" as their eternal habitation (verse 41). As detailed in chapter **4**, these wicked, rebellious angels possess unconditional immortality and therefore must be exiled to exist somewhere for all eternity. What else can God possibly do with such evil, irredeemable creatures that can never die?

Furthermore, Jude 1:7 plainly states that Sodom and Gomorrah were overthrown by "eternal fire." Since these cities have long since been completely incinerated, "eternal fire" in this context must refer to **total destruction which lasts forever** and not never-ending conscious torment. As detailed in chapter **1**, this complete and permanent destruction of Sodom & Gomorrah is a biblical *example* of what will happen to the ungodly when they suffer the second death (2 Peter 2:6). So, technically, the phrase "eternal fire" refers to destruction that lasts forever when applied to human beings. As always, we must resist the temptation to add our own biased interpretation to various biblical phrases and simply let Scripture interpret Scripture.

Mark 9:43-48

Let's turn to another passage often cited to support eternal torment:

> **"If your hand causes you to sin, cut it off. It is better for you to <u>enter life</u> maimed than with two hands to go into hell** *(Gehenna)* **where the fire never goes out.** [45] **And if your foot causes you to sin, cut it off. It is better for you to <u>enter life</u> crippled than to have two feet and be thrown into hell** *(Gehenna).* [47] **And if your eye causes you to sin, pluck it out. It is better for you to enter the kingdom of God with one eye than to have two eyes and be thrown into hell** *(Gehenna),* [48] **where 'their worm does not die, and the fire is not quenched.' "** [23]

> **Mark 9:43-48**

The best way to handle this long passage is to examine it piece by piece and then take it as a whole; but let's first consider three things:

Plainly observe that verses 43 and 45 say that it is better to **enter life** maimed or crippled than to be thrown into "hell," which is *Gehenna* in the Greek. Verse 47 enlightens us that those who "enter life" will "enter the kingdom of God." This is in harmony with what we've repeatedly witnessed in the Scriptures throughout this study: Only the righteous will be granted eternal life and partake of the kingdom of God in the age to come (i.e. the new

---

[23] Verses 44 and 46, which are identical to verse 48, are not found in the best ancient scriptural manuscripts. This explains why modern translations—NIV, NASB, NRSV, etc.—do not include these verses in the main text. Apparently an overzealous scribe intentionally or accidentally repeated these two verses on a later manuscript.

Jerusalem and "new heaven and new earth," as shown in Revelation 21).

If only the righteous will "enter life" in the age to come, then the unrighteous, who will be "thrown into Gehenna" (the lake of fire), will not enter any kind of life at all. On the contrary, they will suffer the second death—everlasting destruction of both soul and body—as we have repeatedly observed.

Secondly, notice that **all three times** Christ refers to the lake of fire in this passage **he uses the example of Gehenna**. As covered in the opening of chapter **2**, Gehenna was the local trash dump & incinerator located right outside the city walls of Jerusalem to the south. Trash, garbage and carcasses of animals, despised criminals & vanquished enemies were thrown into Gehenna for the express purpose of disposal and eradication. Why would Jesus continually use this local trash incinerator as an illustration of the lake of fire? Because Gehenna was a certain **symbol of disposal and eradication** that all of his hearers readily understood. We need to keep this in mind whenever viewing biblical passages that speak of Gehenna. Sadly, many readers will miss out on this important fact because **1.** the English word "hell" disguises the Greek *Gehenna*, and **2.** they lack any historical knowledge of what Gehenna was at the time of Christ' earthly ministry. As such, the myth of hell as never-ending roasting torment is perpetuated.

Thirdly, with the above two points in mind, let's observe Jesus' statement in verse 43: "Hell *(Gehenna), where the fire never goes out.*" This was actually true of Gehenna—the Valley of Hinnom— as the fires of this city dump were kept constantly burning for the purpose of burning up the refuse that was regularly thrown into it. But this is even more so with the lake of fire of which Gehenna is an example. As already covered, Christ spoke of the lake of fire as "the eternal fire **prepared for** the devil and his angels" (Matthew 25:41). The LORD had no choice but to prepare such a place after the devil & his filthy minions rebelled against him. Since the devil & his demons apparently possess unconditional immortality and can never die, the lake of fire will be their eternal habitation; but for mortal human beings, the lake of fire will be used as God's chosen instrument to execute "the second death." The fire never went out in the constantly smoking Valley of Hinnom, but the refuse thrown into it was **eradicated**. The rubbish didn't ludicrously burn forever. In the same way, the fire in the lake of fire will evidently never go out, but the *people* cast in it will be **completely eradicated**.

Gehenna: Where " Their Worm Does Not Die"

Let's now examine Christ's statement in verse 48: "Hell *(Gehenna),* where 'their worm does not die, and the fire is not quenched.' " Despite the obvious ambiguity of this statement, this is one of the major texts cited by adherents of eternal torment to support their view. But, let's be honest here: Does Jesus say anything in this verse about people being in a state of perpetual, undying torment? No. In fact, if we were to take the verse literally Jesus is evidently teaching on the immortality of worms! The case for the eternal torment theory is pretty sad indeed if its adherents must resort to this verse as one of their major proof texts. If the ultimate consequence of sin is as harsh and cruel as everlasting fiery conscious torture, would Jesus Christ, the living Word of God, piddle around making such ambiguous statements? No, he would clearly spell out the truth regarding such an important subject. That's why he plainly referred to the lake of fire as Gehenna *three times* in this very passage, because Gehenna was an unmistakable symbol of destruction that reinforced his many clear and solemn statements regarding the second death.

You'll notice that verse 48 is in quotation marks. That's because Jesus is quoting the very last passage of the book of Isaiah. Although we addressed this verse earlier in the section on Daniel 12:2, let's look at it again from a different translation as this will help us properly interpret Jesus' words:

> **"They** [the righteous] **shall go forth and look on the <u>corpses</u> of the men who have transgressed against me. For their worm shall not die, and their fire shall not be quenched; and they shall be an abhorrence to all mankind."**
>
> **Isaiah 66:24** (NASB)

The "corpses" refer to the people who have transgressed against the LORD and will be thrown into the lake of fire. Please notice that they are **no longer alive**. *They are dead*. They have been **destroyed**. They are loathsome, ashen, worm-chewed **corpses**. They will be "an abhorrence to all mankind" just as an ashen, worm-chewed corpse of a despised criminal would be abhorrent to you or me.

The fact that these transgressors are, in fact, **lifeless corpses** is backed up by verse 16 of the same chapter, which says that they will be "**slain** by the LORD;" and verse 17, which says that "they will **meet their end**." The second death is when the ungodly will **meet their end**, not when they'll meet the beginning of life in never-ending roasting agony.

The Hebrew for "worm" in this verse refers to maggots (Strong 123). The unmistakable fact is that the bodies affected by these maggots are dead. This is fitting since **maggots exclusively devour dead flesh**, not living creatures. And, it should be added, maggots don't die, they pupate and morph into flies.

Being that Gehenna was a garbage dump, maggots bred freely and preyed upon the filth. When corpses of animals or executed criminals were cast in, they would be destroyed by maggots or by the fires that were kept constantly burning there, or a combination of both.

Understanding the unmistakable context of Christ's quote from Isaiah, as well as the historical facts concerning Gehenna, helps us to properly interpret Jesus' words in Mark 9:43-48.

Unfortunately, many misguided preachers who advocate eternal roasting have had a field day with Mark 9:48, conjuring up all kinds of bizarre interpretations, including how immortal worms will forever chew on the undying souls of the damned in the lake of fire. They do this by *not* rightly-dividing the Word of God—ignoring the historical facts about Gehenna and the context of Jesus' quote from Isaiah. They're obviously biased on the subject and, sadly, superficial in their studies. In effect, they're pathetic "yes men" or "yes women" in bondage to the doctrines of their sect regardless of what the Bible actually teaches.

I have a much less ambiguous "worm verse" that I'd like to share, which is also from the book of Isaiah:

> **"For the moth will <u>eat them up like a garment</u>;**
> **the worm will <u>devour them like wool</u>.**
> **But my righteousness will <u>last forever</u>,**
> **my salvation <u>through all generations</u>."**
> **Isaiah 51:8**

Just as moths eat or destroy garments, so the ungodly will be destroyed in the lake of fire. Like Mark 9:48, this is undoubtedly a *figurative* example of everlasting destruction. It is meant to be taken seriously, but not necessarily literally. I doubt, after all, that there will be literal moths or worms in the lake of fire devouring those thrown in. We've already deduced from Scripture that, literally, the ungodly will be *consumed*—both soul and body—by (something akin to) raging fire when cast into the lake of fire. This will result in the blackest darkness of all—absolute obliteration and extinction of being.

Notice how the everlasting destruction of the ungodly is contrasted with the LORD's righteousness and salvation which will **last forever**. Those who accept God's gracious gift of salvation—eternal life—will experience this salvation forever. Those who reject it have no "forever" to look forward to because they will be **destroyed like garments devoured by moths or worms**. Verses 3, 6-8 & 11 also confirm that this is an eschatological passage and therefore relevant to the eternal fate of ungodly people. Why is it that eternal torturists fail to ever mention this "worm verse"? I'll tell you why—it contradicts their religious (but not biblical) position.

Gehenna: Where " the Fire is Not Quenched"

Let's now examine the latter part of verse 48 where Christ says, "hell *(Gehenna)*... where the fire is not quenched." Adherents of eternal torture often attach their own meaning to this statement and suggest that it is supportive of everlasting roasting. However, there are multiple references to unquenchable fire in the Scriptures and none of these passages refer to eternal torment, but rather to fire that cannot be extinguished or resisted and consumes until nothing is left. See for yourself:

> **Therefore this is what the Sovereign LORD says: "My anger and my wrath will be poured out on this place [Judah], on man and beast, on the trees of the field, and on the fruit of the ground, and it will <u>burn and not be quenched</u>."**
> **Jeremiah 7:20**

"Burn and not be quenched" here could not possibly refer to burning forever without end. After all, will the trees of the field and the fruit of the ground, as well as the men and beasts of Judah, burn forever? Obviously not. Here's another example from Jeremiah:

> **"...my wrath will break out and burn like fire**
> **because of the evil you have done—**
> **<u>burn with no one to quench it</u>...**
> **[14] I will punish you as your deeds deserve,"**
> **declares the LORD.**
> **"I will kindle <u>a fire</u> in your forests**
> **that will <u>consume everything around you</u>."**
> **Jeremiah 21:12b,14**

We clearly see here that God's wrath will break out and "burn with no one to quench it" in the sense that it will "**consume everything**."

These and many other passages that mention unquenchable fire prove that such phrases simply refer to the **irrevocability of God's judgment and wrath**—for when the LORD's judgment is pronounced and the fire is set to destroy, He will allow nothing to quench it until the consumption is complete (see, for example, Isaiah 34:9-11, Ezekiel 20:47-48, Amos 5:6, Matthew 3:12 and Luke 3:17).

Finally, let's consider Mark 9:43-48 as a whole. Christ made similar comments in Matthew 5:29-30 and 18:8-9. The point Jesus is making in these passages is clear: If we want to enter eternal life we must be careful to cut off things in our lives that cause us to sin. Why? Because the wages of sin is death and this wage will be meted out in Gehenna, the lake of fire, God's disposal dump & incinerator. In other words, Jesus is encouraging us to flee from sin because unrepentant sin—that is, sin as a lifestyle—will prevent us from entering life, and will, in fact, lead to ultimate extinction. This is a crucial matter that people must grasp. Paul, under the inspiration of the Holy Spirit, made the same point more succinctly when he said, "For the wages of sin is death, but the gift of God is eternal life in Christ Jesus our Lord" (Romans 6:23).

" There Will Be Wrath and Anger... Trouble and Distress"

This next passage is not often cited to support eternal torment, but it has been thrown at me at least once. We need an excuse to look at it anyway as it's actually a good proof text for everlasting destruction:

God "will give to each person according to what he has done." [7] To those who by persistence in doing good, <u>seek</u> glory, honor and <u>immortality</u>, he will give <u>eternal life</u>. [8] But for those who are self-seeking and who reject the truth and follow evil, <u>there will be wrath and anger</u>. [9] <u>There will be trouble and distress</u> for every human being who does evil: first for the Jew, then for the gentile; [10] but glory, honor and peace for everyone who does good: first for the Jew, then for the gentile...

[12] All who sin apart from the law will also <u>perish</u> apart from the law,

Romans 2:6-10, 12

Paul starts out this passage by quoting Psalm 62:12 and Proverbs 24:12: When people are judged, God will give to each according to what he or she has done. To those who persistently do good and **seek immortality,** he will grant **eternal life.** Notice clearly that immortality is not something that people intrinsically possess; no, it's something that must be sought. Those who seek it will find it, as Jesus himself said, "seek and you will find" (Matthew 7:7). We again see that **only one class of people will be granted immortality and eternal life**—those who seek immortality and actively practice their faith, that is, the righteous.[24]

If *only one* of the two classes of people will be granted life and immortality, then we know that the other class will *not* be granted life and immortality. If these people are not granted life and immortality, it naturally follows that they will be condemned to death. That's why Paul goes on to say in verse 12 that all who sin apart from the law will also **perish** apart from the law. As a matter of fact, right before saying this Paul said that, according to God's

---

[24] Remember, the "righteous" are simply those people who are in-right-standing with God because they've let go of *their* fleshly 'righteousness' in acceptance of God's "gift of righteousness" through Christ. See Romans 5:17 and 2 Corinthians 5:21.

righteous decree, those who unrepentantly practice sin **deserve death** (Romans 1:32).

Paul describes the class of people who will not be granted eternal life and immortality, as "self-seeking and who reject the truth and follow evil." He goes on to declare in verses 8 and 9 what this class of people can expect on Judgment Day: "…there will be **wrath and anger**. There will be **trouble and distress**." "Wrath and anger" describe the scene from the LORD's perspective while "trouble and distress" portray it from the viewpoint of those who will suffer God's wrath and anger.

Naturally, adherents of eternal torture would have us believe that God's "wrath and anger" entails never-ending conscious agony. And this is strengthened, they claim, by the proclamation that the recipients will experience "trouble and distress."

There are two obvious problems with this: The first is that it is hermeneutically unsound to take a phrase like "wrath and anger" and add to it our own personal interpretation, which just happens to coincide with our pet beliefs. Secondly, Scripture must always be interpreted by Scripture; this is an interpretational rule because God, the author of Holy Scripture, is of one mind.

So what does God's "wrath and anger" mean according to the Bible? Notice for yourself what results when God's wrath and anger are poured out:

> **"So I will pour out <u>my wrath</u> on them** [the sinful people of Judah] **and <u>consume them with my fiery anger</u>, bringing down on their own heads all they have done, declares the Sovereign LORD."**
> **Ezekiel 22:31**

> [8] **Your hand will lay hold on all your enemies;**
>   **your right hand will seize your foes.**
> [9] **At the time of your appearing**
>   **you will make them like a <u>fiery furnace</u>.**
> **In <u>his wrath</u> the LORD will <u>swallow them up</u>,**

and <u>his fire will consume them</u>.

Psalm 21:8-9

As you can see, when God's wrath and anger are finally poured out—after much patience and mercy, I might add—people are **utterly consumed and destroyed**, not tortured endlessly.

Zephaniah 1:14-2:3 informs us about the future "great day of the LORD" and describes this day as "a day of **wrath**" (1:15,18 & 2:2) and "the day of the LORD's **anger**" (2:2-3). Notice what will result from God's wrath and anger:

> **"Neither their silver nor their gold**
> **will be able to save them**
> **on the day of the LORD's <u>wrath</u>.**
> **In the fire of his jealousy**
> **the whole world will be <u>consumed</u>,**
> **for he will make a <u>sudden end</u>**
> **of all who live on the earth."**

Zephaniah 1:18

Verse 15 describes this day of God's **wrath** and **anger** as "a day of distress" and "a day of trouble" for the recipients of His wrath. Of course they'll experience "trouble and distress," but they won't experience "trouble and distress" continuously forever and ever, as the passage clearly shows that God's wrath and anger will result in the whole world being **consumed**—bringing "a **sudden end** to all who live on the earth."

Because Scripture must always be interpreted in light of what the rest of Scripture teaches, these passages reveal what Paul was talking about in Romans 2:8-9 when he said there will be wrath and anger, trouble and distress for all those who reject the truth and follow evil.

The second reason we cannot take the phrase "there will be wrath and anger… trouble and distress" as a reference to eternal torment is because, as already pointed out, this passage is sandwiched between two crystal clear statements that **1.** according to God's righteous decree, sinners "deserve **death**" (1:32), and **2.** "all who sin apart from the law will also **perish** apart from the law" (2:12). Keep in mind that originally there were no chapter divisions or verse numberings in the epistles; these were added much later for the sake of convenience.

We could sum up Romans 2:6-12 as follows: Only those who "do good" and seek immortality will be granted eternal life. Those who reject the truth and follow evil deserve death and therefore will experience God's wrath and anger, which always results in consumptive perish-ment—"for all who sin apart from the law will also *perish* apart from the law."

Revelation 22:14-15

A couple of people wrote me about this statement Christ makes in the last chapter of the Bible because it sounds as if there will be wicked people right outside the gates of the new Jerusalem in the eternal age of the new heavens and new earth.

Let's read the passage:

> **"Blessed are those who wash their robes, that they may have the right to the tree of life and may go through the gates into the city. [15] <u>Outside are the dogs</u>, those who practice magic arts, the sexually immoral, the murderers, the idolaters and everyone who loves and practices falsehood."**
>
> **Revelation 22:14-15**

Obviously there won't be wicked people just outside the gates of the new Jerusalem because the new heavens and new earth are the "home of **righteousness**" (2 Peter 3:13). It's the place "where **righteousness** dwells," not the place "where righteousness dwells in the city while wickedness dwells without." If damned human beings will be hanging right outside the city gates then that would mean the lake of fire is also right outside the gates, which obviously isn't true. The "new heaven and new earth" refer to the coming eternal age where "There will be no more death or mourning or crying or pain, for the old order of things has passed away"; it's where the LORD makes **everything new** (Revelation 21:5).

The problem lies with the dubious rendering of the Greek text by English translators. The linking verb "are" in the phrase "Outside *are* the dogs" is not in the original text. This is significant because, by adding 'are' to this rendition of the text, it gives the impression that these people will still be alive in the era of the new heavens and new earth. And coupled with the word "outside" it seems like they'll be dwelling right outside the gates of the new Jerusalem.

The Greek for "outside" is *exó*, which means "out, outside, (going) forth or (thrown) away." Adhering to the hermeneutical rule that Scripture interprets Scripture, let's look at a couple of other passages relevant to damnation that also use this word:

> **"Once again, the kingdom of heaven is like a net that was let down into the lake and caught all kinds of fish. [48] When it was full, the fishermen pulled it up on the shore. Then they sat down and collected the good fish in baskets, but threw the bad <u>away</u> *(exó)*. [49] <u>This is how it will be at the end of the age</u>."**
>
> **Matthew 13:47-49**

Christ gave this natural example to illustrate the way it will be with people at the end of this age. What happens to bad fish that are thrown away? Do they exist forever in a state of constant torment or do they suffer for a bit and then perish? Jesus follows up with verses 49-50 where he says that angels will separate the wicked from the righteous at the end of the age and throw the wicked into a "blazing furnace." Being cast into such a furnace indicates nothing other than horrible and total incineration.

This is further emphasized by Jesus' explanation of The Parable of the Weeds in verse 40 of the same chapter: "**As** the weeds are pulled up and burned in the fire, **so it will be** at the end of the age." What happens to weeds cast into fire? Obviously they burn for a little bit, but ultimately **burn up**. Why did Christ use unmistakable illustrations like these? Because they're *unmistakable*. Only a stuffy theologian blinded by sectarianism and tradition could miss their obvious meaning.

Here's a similar passage where *exó* is used in reference to human damnation:

> **"If anyone does not abide in Me, he is thrown away *(exó)* as a branch and dries up; and they gather them, and cast them into the fire and they are burned."**
>
> **John 15:6** (NASB)

Once again, the point cannot be mistaken: The branches are *thrown away* into the fire where they are **burned**. Just like the weeds, the branches **burn up** in the fire; they don't burn forever and ever without quite burning up.

Being "thrown **away** *(exo)*" in these passages is a reference to Gehenna—the Valley of Hinnom—which Christ used as an *example* of the lake of fire or second death (Matthew 10:28). The figurative "fire" is also an obvious reference to the lake of fire. At that time Gehenna was a perpetually smoking trash dump where all manner of refuse was cast for the purpose of disposal and incineration. It's not a pretty picture, but it drives home a powerful point: Those who choose to be God's enemies become God's garbage and will thus be **thrown away**—*exó*—and exterminated, *like* garbage. This was covered in detail in chapter 2.

The comparative Greek word *exóteros (ex-OT-er-us)* is also used by Christ in reference to the lake of fire when he said that the damned would be "thrown **outside**, into the darkness" (Matthew 8:12), covered earlier. So when the Lord says "**Outside** *(exo)* are the dogs" in Revelation 22:14-15 he was saying that they were condemned to the lake of fire, the "second death."

Lastly, the Greek for "practices" in Revelation 22:15 is the verb *poieó (poy-EH-oh)*, which can be past tense, present tense or future tense depending on the context.

All this info helps us translate the original text of Revelation 22:14-15 as such:

> **"Blessed are those who wash their robes, that they may have the right to the tree of life and may go through the gates into the city. [15] Thrown away (in the lake of fire) are the dogs, those who practiced magic arts, the sexually immoral, the murderers, the idolaters and everyone who loved and practiced falsehood."**

Also keep in mind the sequence of events of Revelation chapters 20-22. In 20:11-15 the unrepentant wicked are cast into the lake of fire to suffer the second death. *Then* chapters 21-22 detail the establishment of the new heavens and new earth, the "home of righteousness." The wicked have *already been taken care of* by this point—cast into God's garbage dump and destroyed. Revelation 22:12-21 is the epilogue of Revelation—and the Bible itself—with Christ speaking in verses 12-16 & 20.

" The Smoke of their Torment Rises Forever"

We are left with one last supposed proof text for eternal torture to scrutinize:

> **"If anyone worships the beast and his image and receives his mark on the forehead or on the hand, [10] he, too, will drink of the wine of God's fury, which has been poured out full strength into the cup of his wrath. He will be <u>tormented with burning sulfur in the presence of the holy angels and of the lamb</u> [Jesus]. [11] And <u>the smoke of their torment rises forever and ever. There is no rest day or night</u> for those who worship the**

beast or his image, or anyone who receives the mark of his name."

Revelation 14:9-11

As you can see, this passage describes the harsh divine judgment that will befall people who choose to worship the beast and receive his mark during the Tribulation period. I admit that a casual reading of this text gives the *impression* that these people will suffer eternal roasting torment, but such a conclusion does not stand up to biblical analysis. There are four solid reasons why we cannot interpret this passage as a reference to eternal torture:

First of all, although this passage gives the impression that God will sadistically torment people in his presence forever and ever, **it does not say that**. All it states is that these rebellious people will be tormented with burning sulfur and that "the smoke of their torment rises forever and ever." "Smoke" indicates that they will be burned up and "torment" would refer to the anguish experienced while being burned up. This coincides with what the Holy Spirit inspired David to write in Psalm 37:20: "But **the wicked shall perish**... **Into smoke** they shall **vanish away**" (NKJV).

Earlier we covered the fact that, when people suffer the second death, conscious suffering will be meted out to each individual as divine justice dictates. This makes sense when comparing, say, Jack the Ripper and the friendly pagan guy at work who simply wants nothing to do with the Lord because he loves his pet sin too much. The pagan guy might experience a split second of pain when raging fire consumes him, but doesn't a fiend like Jack the Ripper justly deserve a bit more conscious suffering before eternal oblivion? Of course he does. That's why Christ said Judgment Day would be more bearable for some than for others and that some would be punished more severely even though they all suffer the same ultimate fate—literal everlasting destruction. This is actually a comforting aspect of Judgment Day as every evildoer throughout history who has "gotten away" with wicked deeds will have to stand before the true Supreme Court and answer for his or her crimes. As Erwin Lutzer aptly put it: "Every court case ever tried on earth will be reopened; every action and motive will be meticulously inspected and just retribution meted out. In the presence of an all-knowing God there will be no unsolved murders, no unknown child abductor, and no hidden bribe" (107).

In the case of Revelation 14:9-11, this passage is solely referring to those who have chosen to worship the beast and receive his mark during the Tribulation. This is apparently a heinous sin to God and these people will be punished accordingly.

The second reason we can't take Revelation 14:9-11 as a reference to never-ending torment is because this passage has a "sister text" which uses **the very same terminology** where the meaning can't possibly be mistaken. This sister text is from the Old Testament and is therefore the foundation upon which Revelation 14:9-11 rests:

> **Edom's streams will be turned into pitch,**
> **her dust into <u>burning sulfur</u>;**
> **her land will become <u>blazing pitch</u>!**
> **<u>It will not be quenched night and day</u>;**
> **<u>its smoke will rise forever</u>.**
> **Isaiah 34:9-10a**

Reading this passage we get the impression that the kingdom of Edom will burn forever and ever without end, but the entire rest of the chapter renders this interpretation impossible. The rest of the chapter shows that Edom would become a desolate desert inhabited by owls, jackals and hyenas. Verses 5-6 state that the people of Edom will be "totally destroyed" and slaughtered, and Obadiah 10 & 18 back this up, stating that Edom will "be destroyed forever"—consumed by the fire of God's judgment and wrath. Therefore the statement "it will not be quenched **night and day**; its smoke will rise **forever**" cannot be taken to mean what it might casually appear to mean.

Observe how Isaiah 34:9-10 and Revelation 14:10-11 use the same terminology:

her dust [will be turned] **into <u>burning sulfur</u>**
He will be tormented with <u>burning sulfur</u>

its <u>smoke will rise forever</u>
the <u>smoke</u> of their torment <u>rises forever</u>

It will not be quenched <u>night and day</u>
There is no rest <u>day or night</u>

This shows that the terminology used in Revelation 14:10-11 cannot refer to eternal conscious torment because, just as the entire rest of Isaiah 34 renders this interpretation inaccurate for Isaiah 34:9-10a, **so the entire rest of the Bible renders this interpretation false for Revelation 14:10-11**.

Please notice that Isaiah 34:10 plainly declares that Edom will burn and "not be quenched night and day." This shows that the phrase "night and day" or "day or night" does not refer to an unending amount of time. The burning sulfur that destroyed Edom was not quenched "night and day" until the entire kingdom was destroyed. Likewise, the wicked people spoken of in Revelation 14:10-11 will have no rest from their torment "day or night" until the burning sulfur totally destroys them. "Burning sulfur" is simply another name for the lake of fire (see Revelation 21:8); so being "tormented with burning sulfur" is a reference to the second death. For further proof, Paul said that he worked and prayed "night and day" (1 Thessalonians 2:9; 3:10), but he did neither non-stop; and working ceased when he passed away. Acts 9:24 and Revelation 12:10 give additional support that this phrase refers to a *temporary period of time*.

The third reason we can't regard Revelation 14:10-11 as a reference to eternal fiery torment is because there are other passages in the book of Revelation that also use the terminology used in Revelation 14:10-11, but like Isaiah 34:9-10, these passages distinctly refer to **complete destruction by fire**: Chapter 18 of Revelation deals with the fall of Babylon, which is the result of God's judgment. "Babylon" here prophetically refers to a city that will be the governmental center of the Antichrist's kingdom on earth, likely in Europe and representing a modern version of the old Roman Empire; this is what some scholars maintain. Whatever the case, chapter 18 speaks of "the **smoke** of her **burning**" (verses 9 & 18) and of "her **torment**" (verses 10 & 15), and 19:3 says, "The **smoke from her goes up forever and ever.**" This terminology gives the impression that "Babylon" will be eternally tormented and burn forever and ever, but Revelation 18:8 makes it clear that "She will be **consumed by fire**"—**completely destroyed**—just as this entire present earth will also be destroyed (see 2 Peter 3:10-11). Thus, the statement "the smoke from her goes up forever and ever" can only refer to complete and final destruction.

These passages, which use the terminology of smoke rising forever, coincide with God's total destruction of Sodom & Gomorrah, which is a biblical "example of what is going to happen to the ungodly" at the second death (2 Peter 2:6). In the Genesis account of the destruction of Sodom & Gomorrah, Abraham saw "dense smoke rising from the land, like smoke from a furnace" (19:28).

Fourthly, there's even further reason why we can't take Revelation 14:10-11 as a reference to never-ending roasting torture. Notice clearly from this passage where the tormenting is taking place: "He will be tormented with burning sulfur **in the presence of the holy angels and of the lamb**. And the smoke of their torment rises forever and ever." Being tormented with burning sulfur is referring to suffering the second death (again, Revelation 21:8); according to this passage this "death" will take place **in the presence of God and his holy angels**. So whether we view "tormented with burning sulfur" as a reference to eternal torture or as a reference to the anguish of being completely burned up, it is certain that it will take place **in the very presence of God**. This presents a problem for the view of eternal torment as it shows a God who sadistically tortures his human enemies in his presence forever and ever. Yet it presents no such problem for the view of everlasting destruction as it shows the LORD present at the second death to judge his human enemies and execute their sentence of total, everlasting extermination by his chosen instrument—the lake of fire. As covered in chapter **1**, 2 Thessalonians 1:9 says that ungodly people "shall be punished with everlasting destruction from the presence of the Lord, and from the glory of his power" (KJV) "and shut out from the presence of the Lord and from the majesty of his power" (NIV), *not* **tortured in the presence of the Lord forever and ever**.

In addition, consider the numerous Scriptures that plainly show how there shall be no memory of the ungodly because the Lord will so thoroughly blot out their names forever and ever (see, for example, Psalm 9:5-7, Isaiah 65:16-17 and Obadiah 16). Needless to say, it would be rather hard to forget about the ungodly if they're being tormented in the Lord's presence throughout all eternity. As already examined, Isaiah 66:24 states that the righteous shall "go out and look upon" the carcasses of the damned as worms & fire devour their remains. The faithful will obviously not be able to forget about them until they are totally destroyed, so both Isaiah 66:24 and Revelation 14:9-11 cannot be references to never-ending roasting torment.

As you can see, the claim that Revelation 14:10-11 supports the eternal torment theory does not stand up to a thorough biblical analysis. This shows that it is a mistake to take one or two passages in which we read our own biased meaning into the terminology, disregard the entire rest of the Bible, and try to prove something. It's unsound to do this because **Scripture must always interpret Scripture**; it's a hermeneutical law. After all, I could easily take one or two scriptural texts and "prove" just about anything; that is, as long as I disregard the entire rest of the Bible. For example, I could "prove" that women must remain absolutely silent in the church (1 Corinthians 14:33-38 & 1 Timothy 2:11-14) or that the homosexual lifestyle is okay (2 Samuel 1:26). In both of these cases I was able to come up with what appears to be clear scriptural support to prove my point, yet despite how clear these Scriptures are **by themselves**, in both cases **the entire rest of the Bible renders my casual interpretation false**. Such is the case with Revelation 14:10-11. The terminology used in this passage is used elsewhere in the Bible where it refers to literal everlasting destruction, not eternal torment.

' What about the Rich Man & Lazarus? '

In the previous section I said that Revelation 14:9-11 was the last proof text for eternal torment that was necessary to examine. Some readers might object by pointing out that I failed to address the rich man and Lazarus, an oft-cited support text for eternal torture.

This objection refers to Luke 16:19-31 where Christ tells the story of a rich man and beggar named Lazarus who die and go to "hell" (verse 23). "Hell" in this passage is translated from the Greek word *Hades (HAY-deez)*. Although both the rich man and Lazarus go to Hades in the story, they experience diametrical conditions—the rich man is shown to be in a horrible state of torment whereas the poor man is comforted in "Abraham's bosom." Jesus' 'punchline' for the tale is that some people will not repent and believe even if someone rises from the dead.

It's easy to see why casual Bible readers and non-advanced students might suggest that this passage supports eternal roasting torment. After all, the text portrays the rich man in hell after death and in an obvious state of torment, but let me explain why this story is not relevant to the subject of eternal punishment:

As pointed out above, the word "hell" in this passage is the Greek word *hades* (verse 23). Hades is equivalent to the Hebrew *sheol (sheh-OHL)*. Sheol/Hades refers to the intermediate state of the soul between decease and resurrection and is therefore **a *temporary* condition** (Vine 286).

Since Sheol/Hades does not refer to the lake of fire, it's obviously **not relevant to the subject of *eternal* punishment in the lake of fire**, which is the subject of this book.

There are differing views concerning the nature of Sheol/Hades. For instance, is it a place where souls exist in conscious torment (or comfort, as was the case with Lazarus)? Or is it a well of "sleeping" (i.e. dead) souls awaiting resurrection? In other words, is it simply the condition of death itself—"the graveyard of souls" in the heart of the earth—where souls are extinct as far as conscious life goes; and their remains are 'awaiting' resurrection? *Sheol* appears 66 times in the Old Testament and *Hades* appears 10 times in the New Testament. There are numerous other scriptural references to Sheol/Hades as well (like "pit" and "the land of silence"). A prayerful, thorough and unbiased examination of these numerous passages will clearly reveal the truth and I encourage you to do such a study. In fact, this is the very purpose of my book *SHEOL KNOW*.

Regardless of what view one accepts concerning this "intermediate state" of the unsaved, the fact of the matter is that biblical passages referring to Sheol/Hades are **not relevant to the subject of eternal punishment**—i.e. **the everlasting fate of ungodly people**. Needless to say, it is absolutely erroneous to take passages that refer to Sheol/Hades—like Luke 16:19-31—and teach on eternal punishment. Unfortunately, but to be expected, many adherents of eternal torment habitually use Luke 16:19-31 for this very purpose, no doubt due to the lack of legitimate texts to support their position. Those who make a practice of this—such as Norman Geisler and Robert Peterson—do so to their own shame.

The bottom line is this: Whether you regard the story of the rich man and Lazarus as a literal historical account or as a symbolic parable, **it is not pertinent to the subject of this study**. See the article on this parable at the Fountain of Life site and my book *SHEOL KNOW* for details.

"Rightly Dividing the Word of Truth"

Taking the story of the rich man and Lazarus and using it as a proof text for never-ending torment is a good example of "*un*rightly dividing" the Scriptures. To explain, let's view a verse that instructs us on proper scriptural study and interpretation:

> **<u>Study</u> to show thyself <u>approved unto God</u>, a workman that needeth not to be ashamed, <u>rightly dividing the word of truth</u>.**
> **2 Timothy 2:15** (KJV)

Notice that we are encouraged to "study." This means that our interpretation of the Scriptures should *not* be based on superficial observation, but upon *a thorough examination wherein we interpret Scripture with Scripture,* which is precisely what we've been doing in this study. As long as we do this, and we're honest with the Scriptures—letting go of all biases—the truth should be plain to see on any given subject. This is called "rightly dividing the word of truth," which simply means to handle it correctly (see the NIV translation of the passage).

If it is possible to "rightly divide" the Scriptures it is also unfortunately possible to "*un*rightly divide" them. We've seen in this study that a thorough examination of the Word of God strongly supports the view of everlasting destruction; but a person could very easily "*un*rightly divide" the Scriptures and 'prove' that the Bible supports eternal torture. All they have to do is take a handful of passages where they add their own biased meaning instead of properly allowing Scripture to interpret Scripture. We observed examples of this in this chapter. Another example would be to take a passage and misapply it, as would be the case with the parable of the rich man and Lazarus. Even if we were to take this story literally it would still only refer to the temporary state between physical decease and resurrection; it therefore cannot be applied as a reference to the second death, which concerns the *eternal fate* of the ungodly.

Needless to say, watch out for those who unrightly divide the Scriptures!

Conclusion on Claimed Support Texts for Eternal Fiery Torture

This ends our examination of the smattering of passages that eternal torturists cite to validate their doctrine. A careful biblical examination has shown that *none* of these passages actually support this false teaching; as a matter of fact, they actually provide further evidence for literal everlasting destruction. Revelation 14:9-11 is their most promising text but, as we have seen, the terminology contained in this passage is used elsewhere in Scripture where it clearly refers to literal destruction that lasts forever and not never-ending roasting torment.

6

EXTRA-BIBLICAL
Arguments for Eternal Torture

In light of the overwhelming biblical support for literal everlasting destruction and the lack thereof for eternal torment, adherents of the latter position have resorted to all manner of bizarre religious theories and objections. This chapter examines the most popular extra-biblical arguments from adherents of never-ending roasting torment.

Let's start with their two favorite arguments...

'Death Means "Separation"'

There are doctrinal "sacred cows" in Christendom that aren't actually biblical. One of these is the curious theory that death doesn't really mean death at all, but rather "separation."

Consider Paul's unmistakable statement in this passage:

> **For the wages of sin is <u>death</u> *(thanatos)*, but the gift of God is eternal life in Christ Jesus our Lord.**
>
> **Romans 6:23**

"Death" here is translated from the Greek word *thanatos (THAYN-ah-tohs),* which simply means "death" (Strong 35)—the absence of life or opposite of life. Greek scholar E.W. Bullinger says that *thanatos* refers to "The natural end of life" (207). Although this is simple to understand and commonly understood, those who teach that human damnation consists of eternal (perpetual) torment "explain" that death in this passage doesn't really mean death, but rather "separation from God." When you press them for details as to exactly what they mean by "separation from God," it turns out that they really mean never-ending conscious life in fiery torment. Do you see the obvious problem with this theory? Under the guise of "interpretation" they would have us believe that death actually means *the exact opposite of what it really is!* In other words, since "the wages of sin" to them is not death at all, but rather immortal life in conscious torment, their definition of death means something entirely opposite to literal death! If this isn't a blatant example of subtracting from God's Word and adding to it, I don't know what is.

This religious theory must be rejected for a number of obvious reasons:

1. If we take "eternal life" literally, we must also take "death" literally

God clearly declares in Romans 6:23 above, as well as numerous other passages, that the wages of sin is death and eternal life is a gift to those in right-standing with him. So death is promised as a punishment for impenitent rebels and life is promised as a gift for the righteous. In such a context as this, every law of language and common sense agrees that if we take the promise of life literally we must also take the punishment of death literally. If one is literal then both are literal. If there is to be no real death for unrepentant sinners there will be no real life for repentant saints.

Adherents of eternal torment can insist that death only means "separation" all they want, but the simple fact is that **the opposite of life is death**. What word could better describe the end of life than 'death'? The only way a person can accept the view of eternal torture is to believe that death doesn't mean death, that die doesn't mean die, that destroy doesn't mean destroy, that perish doesn't mean perish, that destruction doesn't mean destruction and that consume doesn't mean consume.

2. Physical death is death of the body

While most Christians believe the soul (mind & spirit) survives the body, we cannot ignore the biblical fact that "the body without the spirit is dead" (James 2:26). The body is not itself separated; it is **dead**. It no longer has life in it because death is the opposite of life. Death means death, it's not complicated. *Thanatos,* the Greek word translated as death in Romans 6:23 above, is used most often simply in reference to this death, the first death. For example:

> **"I found that the accusation had to do with questions about their law, but there was no charge against him** [Paul] **that deserved <u>death</u>** *(thanatos)* **or imprisonment."**
>
> **Acts 23:29**

The Roman commander speaking in this verse is merely attesting that Paul committed no crime worthy of execution or imprisonment. *Thanatos* here simply refers to **physical execution—the cessation of physical life**. When a person is executed his/her conscious life expires, at least as far as physical life is concerned. Believe it or not, adherents of eternal torture suggest that "death" refers to separation even in this context. Their theory is that death would refer to separation of the inner being (mind & spirit) from the outer being (body) (Dake 619). According to this theory the Roman commander really meant to say, "There was no charge against Paul that deserved separation of the inner being from the outer being or imprisonment." Did the Roman commander really mean to say this when he used the word *thanatos?* Of course not, the idea is ludicrous. The usage of *thanatos* here refers to literal physical death, the expiration of conscious life in the body. This is how James 2:26 above defines physical death: **the body without the spirit is dead**. That is, **void**

of conscious life. Whether or not a person's consciousness exists on a spiritual plane after physical death is another issue.

3. The same biblical words used in reference to the second death are also used in reference to the death of animals

In his popular lexicon (a dictionary of biblical words), W.E. Vine admits that *thanatos*—death—*is* indeed "the opposite of life," but then completely contradicts this statement by saying that "it never denotes non-existence" (Vine 149). With all due respect, Mr. Vine would do well to forsake his sectarian bias and honestly dig a little deeper in his studies as the Scriptures blatantly disagree with this statement. Case in point: The equivalent Hebrew word for death, *maveth (MAW-veth)* (see 1 Corinthians 15:54-55, which combines quotes from Isaiah 25:8 and Hosea 13:14 supplanting the Hebrew *maveth* with the Greek *thanatos*). *Maveth* is used in reference to the death of animals in the Old Testament:

> **Man's fate is like that of the animals; the same fate awaits them both: as one <u>dies</u>** *(maveth)* **so <u>dies</u>** *(maveth)* **the other.**
> **Ecclesiastes 3:19**

> **As <u>dead</u>** *(maveth)* **flies give perfume a bad smell, so a little folly outweighs wisdom and honor.**
> **Ecclesiastes 10:1**

Would anyone ludicrously argue that the equivalent Hebrew word for death in these verses refers to "separation" or never-ending torment? Of course not. Animals and flies that experience death *(thanatos/maveth)* literally die—their life ceases. They of course leave behind a dead, decaying shell, but their conscious life expires. That's what death is. It's plain and simple. This disproves Vine's unscholarly theory as animals definitely cease to exist when they die, that is, their conscious life expires. If "death" *(thanatos/maveth)* literally means death when used in reference to animals, why would its definition mysteriously change to something completely different—actually opposite—when applied to human beings? It doesn't, but adherents of eternal torment are forced to interpret the Bible in this bizarre manner because of their unbiblical theology. (Their reasoning is: "If people have an immortal soul and can therefore never actually die, then death can't really mean death when used in reference to people").

4. Numerous other biblical words besides *thanatos* describe the second death in strict terms of death and destruction

As we've seen throughout this study, *thanatos* is supported by many other Hebrew and Greek words which are variously translated as "die," "death," "destruction," "destroy," "perish" and "consume" in reference to the fate of those cast into the lake of fire. As covered in the first three chapters, these words are backed-up by numerous crystal clear **examples** of literal destruction, like weeds thrown into fire (Matthew 13:40), a king's enemies being *executed* in front of him (Luke 19:27) and the very word for "hell" itself, Gehenna—a symbolic reference to the lake of fire, which is the second death. Add to this the fact that the Bible says point blank that **eternal life and immortality are only available through the gospel** (2 Timothy 1:10 & Romans 2:7). In light of all these factors, even **if** *thanatos* had a secondary definition of "separation" — which it doesn't — it still wouldn't refer to separation in regards to the second death of human beings.

5. If the fate of ungodly sinners is to be some sort of life or "existence" in undying "separation" from God in misery and torment, God would have certainly expressed this repeatedly in the Bible

He could have easily chosen words to describe damnation in explicit terms of "separation," "existence in torment" or "perpetual life in misery," but He did not do this. Forgive me for being redundant, but God consistently chose words that have for their usual, basic meaning "die," "death," "destruction," "destroy," "perish," "consume" and "burn up." This was established in chapter 1. **God couldn't possibly use a better choice of words to describe literal death.** He then made sure to back-up these unmistakable words with multiple easy-to-understand *examples* of literal death and incineration, as noted above and in detail in chapter 2.

Consider also that if *thanatos* really meant "separation" then why should English Bible translators even bother translating *thanatos* as "death" at all (which they unanimously do)? Why not rather universally translate it as "separation"? Wouldn't this simplify matters and spare us all a lot of confusion? The obvious reason they don't do this is because *thanatos* literally means death, the opposite of life, and therefore non-existence or, we could say, the state of non-being. **Death is not a different form of life; it is the opposite of life.** Thus the first death, which is physical death, refers at least to non-existence in the physical realm; and the second death—which entails the everlasting destruction of soul and body—refers to absolute non-existence with no hope of resurrection.

6. "Death" and "separation" are two completely different words in Hebrew and Greek, just as they are in English; these words have different meanings

The Hebrew *badal (baw-DAL)* and the Greek *chorizo (koh-RID-zoh)* are two Old and New Testament words for "separation" (see, for example, Isaiah 59:2 and Romans 8:35,39). If the wages of sin is not really death, but rather separation, then God would have used these Hebrew and Greek words to describe the ultimate wages of sin. For example, Romans 6:23 would read, "For the wages of sin is separation *(chorizo)*" and Ezekiel 18:4 would read, "The soul who sins will separate *(badal)*." But does the Bible teach this anywhere? No, "the wages of sin is death" and "the soul who sins will die" (NASB).

It is true that one of the *results of* sin is separation from God (Isaiah 59:2). This is spiritual death, which simply means that **one's spirit is dead to God**. Those who are spiritually dead cannot have a relationship with the LORD because God is spirit, and those who worship and know the Creator can only do so in spirit and in

> **I warn everyone who hears the words of the prophecy of this book: If anyone <u>adds</u> anything, God will add to him the plagues described in this book. [19] And if anyone takes words away from this book of prophecy, God will take away from him his share in the tree of life and in the holy city, which are described in this book.**
>
> **Revelation 22:18-19**

As you can see, it's a grave offense in God's eyes to subtract from his Word and add to it something else. As pointed out in Proverbs 30 above, the God-breathed Scriptures are flawless. There's simply no reason to make any changes. But adherents of eternal torment are guilty of this transgression in regards to the Bible's repeated declaration that the wages of sin is death.

The scriptural arguments above are proof enough that 'death' simply means death in the Bible and not "separation," but here's additional proof...

8. A comparison of New Testament words for "death," "perish," "destruction," etc. to other well-known Greek writings of the same general period offers additional support

For example, Plato argued that the human soul is immortal and can never die or cease to exist. What Greek words did Plato use to express this denial? He used the exact Greek words that Paul and others in the New Testament used to describe the everlasting destruction of unbelievers. Here are several examples to show what I mean: Plato taught that the human soul would not die *(apothnesko),* Paul taught that it could die (e.g. Romans 8:13); Plato taught that the human soul would never experience death *(thanatos),* Paul and James taught that it could experience death (e.g. James 5:20); Plato taught that the human soul would not suffer destruction *(apoleia* and *olethros),* Paul, Peter and Christ taught that it could suffer destruction (e.g. 2 Thessalonians 1:9, 2 Peter 3:7 and Matthew 7:13-14).

Plato used these various Greek words to describe absolute extinction of being, not separation of being. Since Paul and others used these very same words to describe the eternal fate of those who reject God's message of reconciliation in Christ, we must conclude that they too were referring to absolute extinction of being (Constable 42).

Furthermore, there were people in the 1st Century who adhered to universal extinction, that is, they believed that when people died they simply ceased to exist, with no hope of resurrection for either the righteous or unrighteous. The Epicureans were Greeks who advocated this view and the Sadducees were Jews who supported it. What words did these sects use to express their belief in absolute extinction of conscious life? Why, the very same Greek words used in the New Testament to describe the everlasting destruction of the ungodly (Constable 48).

So, death simply meant death in uninspired writings—the cessation of life—just as it does in the biblical Scriptures.

In light of these eight reasons, we have no recourse but to take God at his Word and conclude that the second death will be a literal death—utter, awful, complete and final. The religious theory that death means "separation" must be categorically rejected.

'What about Spiritual Death?'

This next objection goes hand in hand with the argument that death means "separation." Under the guise of "interpretation" many sincere Christians add the word "spiritual" to the numerous plain passages that promise death to unrepentant sinners. For instance, they argue that Romans 6:23 should read: "For the wages of sin is *spiritual* death, but the gift of God is eternal life in Christ our Lord." They then translate 'spiritual death' as "eternal separation from God because of sin" (Dake 619). The obvious problem with doing this is that **none of the multitude of biblical texts that promise death and destruction as the ultimate wage of sin contain the word "spiritual."**

God wrote the Scriptures through men by the Holy Spirit (2 Peter 1:20-21 & 2 Timothy 3:16). The Bible is truly "God's Word." If the LORD really meant to say "spiritual death" in all these passages we've looked at throughout this study then God would've said so. I don't think the Almighty needs our help in writing a book, do you?

Actually, adding the word "spiritual" to the numerous passages that promise death to unrepentant sinners is another case of adding to God's word and subtracting what it really says—a practice that's condemned in the Scriptures, as already noted.

Speaking of which, earlier in this chapter we observed that spiritual death is a legitimate doctrine. To understand spiritual death it's necessary to understand that people "connect" with God through the spiritual side of their nature. Thus **spiritual death simply means that the spirit of a person is dead to God, that is, the capacity of his/her spirit to unite or commune with God is dead**. "Original sin" is the reason this capacity does not exist. In order for a person's spirit to unite with God he or she has to be spiritually regenerated. This explains why Jesus taught that our spirit must be "born again" for us to "see the kingdom of God" (John 3:3-6).[25]

So spiritual death is a *present state* of the non-Christian. This is why Paul described the Ephesians as "dead in transgressions" *before* their spiritual rebirth (Ephesians 2:5). The second death, by contrast, is a *future event* entailing the complete destruction of soul and body in hell. So **spiritual death ultimately results in the second death**, which is an **absolute death**. This death is described in the Bible as "everlasting destruction" (2 Thessalonians 1:9) and the destruction "of soul and body" (Matthew 10:28) wherein "raging fire will consume the enemies of God" (Hebrews 10:26-27,31). This occurs when the unrepentant wicked are discarded in the lake of fire "which is the second death" (Revelation 20:11-15).

---

[25] The doctrine of "original sin" suggests that humanity's fallen nature—our inclination to commit sin—was naturally passed on to all of us by our primeval parents, Adam and Eve.

All the relevant passages we've examined in this study apply to the second death, a future event. None of them refer to spiritual death, which is a present state in the non-believer's life.

' When you Burn Something, It Simply Changes Form '

H. Buis pointed out that adherents of everlasting destruction place great emphasis on the fact that the figure of "fire" is used in the Bible to describe the second death, "and fire, they point out, always destroys... But the fact is that when you burn something it is not annihilated, it simply changes form" (Buis 125). I guess what Mr. Buis is trying to say is that when, say, a log is burned up, it technically isn't wiped out from existence; it turns to smoke vapors and ashes. While this is true, the simple fact is that **the log itself is destroyed—it no longer exists**. The smoke vapors and ashes are merely the *remains* of the log.

The same is true when God "destroys both soul and body in hell *(Gehenna)."* Concerning the body, when it is destroyed the remains will simply return to the dust from which it came (Genesis 3:19 & Psalm 146:4). As for the soul, no one knows what spiritual materials God creates a soul from but, whatever they are, when the soul is destroyed it will return to such. The simple fact is that the soul is destroyed, just like the log, regardless of what materials it reverts to after its destruction.

Incidentally, in light of the creation text, Genesis 2:7, which says that the soul and body are animated by a "breath of life" from God, some might wonder what happens to this "breath of life" when the soul is destroyed. Well, according to this creation text, it is the breath of life from God that makes the soul "a living soul." When the soul is destroyed, the breath of life simply returns to God who gave it (see Ecclesiastes 12:7, Psalm 146:4, Job 34:14-15 and 1 Maccabees 2:62-63). Naturally, a soul without God's animating breath of life is a *dead* soul.

Throughout this study we've seen that the only words used to describe the destruction of soul and body in hell *(Gehenna)* are "die," "death," "destruction," "destroy," "perish," "consume," and "burn up." The meaning of these terms can be comprehended by children; we don't need to become advanced physicists to understand their obvious meaning.

I should add that literal destructionism is not the belief that the remains of the body and soul cease to exist when people suffer the second death; it is the contention that their conscious life expires. In other words, it's the conscious life of their being that is annihilated not whatever substances God used to create their being. The simple fact is that God is the Creator of all things, including human beings; and whatever he creates he can just as easily **de-create**, that is, **destroy**.[26] Why do eternal torturists find this so difficult to grasp?

' Torment is Not Torture '

You may have noticed that I regularly refer to the view of eternal torment as eternal torture. Both apply to the same position—never-ending conscious suffering.

Norman Geisler, a staunch adherent of eternal torment, objects to using torment and torture interchangeably. His contention is that hell, the lake of fire, is indeed a place of torment, but it is not a realm of torture for "unlike torture, which is inflicted from without against one's will, torment is self-inflicted."[27] Mr. Geisler is a great man of God and I highly recommend his works — I want to stress this — but this argument is both nonsensical and unbiblical.

I have no idea where Geisler got this definition for torment—that it is always self-inflicted—but it certainly wasn't the Bible. For

---

[26] The only exception to this, as detailed in chapter 4, would be beings that willingly accept God's gift of intrinsic immortality, such as all angelic beings. This will include redeemed human beings after their resurrection unto eternal life; see Luke 20:34-36.

[27] From *Everything You Wanted to Know about Hell*, 34.

example, Revelation 11:10 details how two prophets will "torment those who live on the earth" during the Tribulation. This torment is not self-inflicted at all as it obviously comes from an outside source. Also, consider the fact that the King James Version and the New International Version both use "torment" and "torture" interchangeably. See for yourself by looking up these passages in both versions: Matthew 8:29, Mark 5:7 and Revelation 9:5.

Obviously Geisler has a problem with the word "torture" being used to describe his belief in the never-ending conscious misery of unredeemed people. The reason I use the word "torture" to describe this belief is to expose the doctrine for what it really is. Let's be honest enough to call a spade a spade!

Consider this illustration: If I tied a man to a chair and tormented him for five minutes with a lighter, would this not be torture? Of course it would. Subjecting a person to torment *is* torture. How much more so the prospect of subjecting a person to everlasting fiery torment?

But Geisler argues that eternal torment in the lake of fire is self-inflicted—living with the consequences of one's bad choices—and therefore it's not torture. This is more unbiblical mumbo jumbo. God Himself is going to forever destroy people who choose sin and reject his gift of salvation (Matthew 10:28, Hebrews 10:26-27,31 & James 4:12). Regardless of what "destroy" really means—whether literal destruction or eternal torment—the fact is that it is **God Himself who is doing the destroying or, at least, doing it in the sense of authorizing it**. Therefore everlasting destruction is not self-inflicted at all; it is executed by the LORD as the just consequences of a person's bad choices.

This is actually a merciful action on God's part. How so? If a person unrepentantly rebels against the LORD and makes himself or herself miserable through sin—usually spreading misery to others as well—the kindest, most merciful thing God can do is to let such a person die. Then this stubborn, foolish person will be unable to bring further misery to himself/herself or others.

Why does Geisler have such a problem with the word "torture" as a descriptive term for his belief in never-ending conscious torment? What has compelled him to create his own personal and unbiblical definition for "torment" (i.e. that it is only self-inflicted)? The answer is obvious and offers proof that the idea of eternal torment is indeed a profoundly disturbing concept that naturally offends our God-given moral and judicial instincts: The only way Geisler and like-minded people can accept this idea and live with themselves is by convincing themselves that their good, loving God is not the one carrying out (or authorizing) this sadistic sentence.

Is Endless Torture Better than Merciful Death?

Let's observe another one of Mr. Geisler's arguments in defense of eternal torture:

> *Annihilation would demean both the love of God and the nature of human beings as free moral creatures. It would be as if God said to them, "I will allow you to be free only if you do what I say. If you don't, then I will snuff out your very freedom and existence!" This would be like a father telling his son he wanted him to be a doctor, but when the son chose to be a park ranger the father shot him. Eternal suffering is eternal testimony to the freedom and dignity of humans, even unrepentant humans (from Christian Apologetics, 22).*

There are a number of problems with Mr. Geisler's argument. For one, he says that the view of literal destruction (which he calls "annihilation") snuffs out the very freedom of people. Is he ludicrously trying to convince us that locking people in a colossal chamber of endless torments is freedom? Need I say more?

Secondly, Geisler's parable of the son who goes against his father's wishes by choosing to be a ranger instead of a doctor is completely unfitting. The son is supposed to represent a rebellious sinner worthy of the judgment of eternal damnation. Since when is simply deciding on an occupation an evil thing? How can this be comparable to a person whom the Almighty justly deems worthy of eternal death? Rejecting God's gift of reconciliation and eternal life in favor of sin bears absolutely no resemblance to merely choosing an occupation. Also, the symbolism of God as a father who damns his son simply because the son chooses an occupation against his wishes is wholly inappropriate. For one thing, our heavenly Father is an absolute authority whereas earthly fathers have very limited authority. They have the right to advise and influence their children on occupational options but they certainly don't have the authority to assign them an occupation and kill them if they refuse. I could elaborate but it's not worth it.

Thirdly, notice that Geisler fails to apply his little parable to the religious notion of eternal torture. Disregarding the inappropriate symbolism of his tale, let's go ahead and do this for him:

> *If the doctrine of eternal roasting torment were true it would be like a father telling his son he wanted him to be a doctor, but when the son chooses to be a park ranger the father locks him in a large oven and subjects him to ceaseless torture day and night. The father is sure to never allow his son to sleep or mercifully die; he makes sure to keep him alive and awake enough to always feel the painful torment and cry out in agony, year after year, decade after decade, on and on and on and on.*

Why did Geisler fail to share his parable in this manner? After all, if he can apply the tale to the view of literal destruction it's only right that he should apply it to eternal torture as well. The obvious reason he failed to do this is because it exposes his belief as the sham that it is.

Now, again, I completely reject the symbolism of this story; our Creator should not be compared to a father who savagely punishes his son because he merely chooses an occupation with which he disagrees. But, supposing the symbolism is valid and just, which scenario is more sadistic—to mercifully execute or to torment endlessly? Which scenario is the depth of human perversion?

Executing a person is a severe enough punishment, but to ceaselessly torture a person is horribly twisted and repulsive—moral degeneracy of the lowest depth. This is regardless of how guilty the individual is.

Lastly, Geisler is attempting to prove that subjecting people to never-ending conscious torment is more just and moral than putting them to death. Eternal torture is better than merciful death? I find it hard to believe that anyone would even attempt to convince people of this.

'Hell is Where You Can Do Your Own Thing— Forever'

Let's examine Mr. Geisler's weakest argument in defense of never-ending torment, albeit you'll be hard-pressed to find any torment or suffering in this description of damnation:

> One of the reasons there's a hell [i.e. eternal torment] is because God is so loving that He won't force people to do anything against their will... He loves people so much that He will say to them, "You don't want to worship me? You don't want to praise me? You don't want to come to my place? Do your own thing." In other words, **hell is a place where people can do their own thing forever.**

How's this for a completely watered-down version of the traditional concept of damnation? If people are truly free to "do their own thing" in the lake of fire, as Geisler suggests, then they'd at least have to have as much freedom as they have here on earth. So basically we're talking about a life very similar to the life we know on earth with the exceptions that God and death will be of no concern. So hell, according to Geisler, is doing whatever you want forever without ever having to worry about God, judgment, aging or dying. Frankly, this sounds like a pagan paradise more than anything else. If Christians described damnation to people like this do you think they'd ever care to get saved? No, they'd more likely get excited about going to hell and having a never-ending party truth (see John 4:24). That's why Christ taught that we need to have a spiritual rebirth in order to know God (John 3:3-6; see also Titus 3:5). Jesus experienced separation from the Father when he bore our sins on the cross. He even cried out, "My God, my God, why have you forsaken me?" (Matthew 27:46). He also experienced severe suffering when he was crucified. While it was horrible for Christ to experience this separation and suffering, it ended in death. The penalty Jesus paid for our sins was **separation from God, temporary suffering, followed by death**. This was an *example* of the second death to all humanity. Those who are already separated from God (i.e. spiritually dead) and reject the LORD's offer of reconciliation can likewise expect suffering that ends in death on Judgment Day (Revelation 20:11-15).

The bottom line is that the second death is consistently described in terms of literal death and utter destruction in the Bible, not "separation."

7. To suggest that death means something entirely opposite of its actual definition is a blatant case of subtracting from God's Word and adding to it

Adherents of eternal torment subtract the word "death" *(thanatos)* from the numerous passages which describe the wages of sin strictly in terms of literal death, and supplant it with "eternal life in separation from God" — a definition that is, once again, completely opposite to the actual definition of death. This practice is all done under the noble mask of "interpretation," but notice how the Bible strictly condemns this practice:

> **<u>Do not add</u> to what I command you and do not subtract from it, but keep the commands of the LORD your God that I give you.**
> **Deuteronomy 4:2**

> **Every word of God is flawless;...**
> **⁶ <u>Do not add</u> to his words,**
> **or he will rebuke you and prove you a liar.**
> **Proverbs 30:5-6**

with their buddies (which, of course, is how many unbelievers make light of the notion of eternal damnation). By contrast, Christ solemnly declared that hell is a terrifying reality and that we should fear God who has the authority to cast us there:

> **"I tell you, my friends, do not be afraid of those who kill the body and after that can do no more.**
> **⁵ But I will show you whom you should fear: Fear Him who, after the killing of the body, has power to throw you into hell** *(Gehenna)***. Yes, I tell you, fear Him."**
>
> **Luke 12:4-5**

Geisler's idea that hell is a place where people can do their own thing forever doesn't remotely fit the solemn biblical warnings of the second death; in fact, his belief makes an utter absurdity of it. To illustrate, let's interpret Jesus' statement in verse 5 according to Geisler's view:

> "Fear Him who, after the killing of the body, has power to throw you into hell where you'll be free to do whatever you want for all eternity without any moral responsibility to your Creator. Yes, I tell you, fear Him."

It simply makes no sense to fear God if his ultimate punishment for sinners is to merely allow them to do their own thing forever. Do you see how ridiculously off-track people can get when they veer from the plain truth of God's Word? It's so unscriptural it's utterly heretical.

One might argue that I'm taking Geisler too literally here, but if he doesn't really believe this is an accurate description of damnation then why would he teach it? This is especially so considering he made the statement on a television program that would reach millions of people—A&E's *Mysteries of the Bible* segment "Heaven and Hell." Watch the episode yourself and you'll see that he's absolutely serious. Geisler does go on to briefly mention the torment that people will endure while "doing their own thing forever" but, as previously pointed out, his idea of torment is merely living with the consequences of one's bad choices.

Geisler is naturally forced to come up with unbiblical nonsense like this because the traditional concept of never-ending conscious torment is so monstrously evil and unscriptural that he has no other choice. When theologians have to resort to such ridiculous and unbiblical arguments as this it's a sure sign that a doctrine is in its death throes. Our study on the nature of the second death has clearly shown that this fantastical image of damnation is wholly foreign to the Scriptures.

' A Spirit, by Definition, Cannot Die '

Some oppose literal destruction on the grounds that people are spiritual beings, and "By definition, a spirit cannot die. A spirit is an immortal being" (Robertson 72).

You'll notice that anyone who makes such an argument will fail to quote any biblical passages to support this definition. That's because there are none. Nor does a standard English dictionary support it. The Funk & Wagnall's dictionary defines 'spirit' as "A supernatural and immaterial being." A spirit is an immaterial being, that's all. This doesn't mean an immaterial being is unable to die.

It's as simple as this: **Whatever creature God gives life to he can bring death to. Whatever he creates he can also de-create.** The human mind or disembodied soul did not always exist; it was created by God out of immaterial substances and given consciousness by God's "breath of life." And the simple fact is that whatever is created can be de-created, that is, destroyed. If the LORD justly decides that a human being is worthy of death—soul and body—he certainly has the power to do it; after all, he's the One who created human beings. Jesus Christ Himself declared that this is exactly what God will do to people on Judgment Day when they're cast into the lake of fire (Matthew 10:28).

The exception would be creatures who possess God's gift of unconditional immortality, specifically the devil & his filthy angels. God will one day grant unconditional immortality to people as well, but only those who have been redeemed through spiritual rebirth in Christ. Such people will have "the right to the tree of life" and live forever (see Revelation 22:14,19 and 2:7). As for unredeemed human beings, the LORD refuses to grant such people this right because they'd have to exist forever in a miserable fallen state, like the fallen angels. Needless to say, unconditional immortality as such would be a curse. This is why, after Adam sinned and spiritually died, God said: "He must not be allowed to reach out his hand and take also from the tree of life and eat, and *live forever*" (Genesis 3:22). The LORD therefore denied Adam access to the tree of life (verses 23-24). This was covered in detail in chapter 4.

Human beings presently have yet to attain unconditional immortality and therefore are mercifully subject to literal death and destruction as justly deemed by the Almighty.

' You are Confusing "Eternal Life" with "Eternal Existence" '

An adherent of eternal torture presented this argument:

> *You are confusing "eternal life" with "eternal existence." The orthodox view is that we all have eternal existence, but only in Christ do believers receive eternal life. All others are left in their natural state of eternal death.*

The problem with this argument is that there's no biblical Greek or Hebrew word for "existence" beyond the words for "life" detailed in this book—*zoe* and *chay*—and their derivatives. This explains why the man didn't cite any such Hebrew or Greek word.

Secondly, you'll notice that he fails to cite any passages to support his position. That's because there aren't any. The Bible point blank says that eternal life and immortality are only available to people *through* the message of Christ:

> **...our Savior, Christ Jesus, who has destroyed death and has <u>brought life and immortality to light through the gospel</u>.**
> **2 Timothy 1:10**

The only life (*zoe*) that unredeemed people possess is the ***temporal*** life (*zoe*) inherited from Adam, which God "gives all men" (Acts 17:25). To inherit *eternal* life (*zoe*) we must be **born again of the imperishable seed of Christ**, the second Adam. This is what the gospel of Christ is all about. As it is written:

> **For as in Adam all die, so <u>in Christ all will be made alive</u>.**
> **1 Corinthians 15:22**

> **For you have been born again, not of perishable seed, but of <u>imperishable</u>, through the living and enduring word of God.**
> **1 Peter 1:23**

This helps us to understand why Jesus said we must be "born again" to see the kingdom of God in John 3:3,6. Christ goes on to say: "For God so loved the world that he gave his one and only Son, that whoever believes in him shall **not perish** but **have eternal life**." Please notice that Jesus *doesn't* say "whoever believes in him shall not have eternal existence but have eternal life." This renders the text baffling, to say the least. Furthermore, John 3 goes on to say: "Whoever believes in the Son has eternal life, but whoever rejects the Son **will not see life**, for God's wrath remains on them" (verse 36). Observe that it *doesn't* say: "Whoever believes in the Son has eternal life, but whoever rejects the Son will have eternal existence." Needless to say, the eternal torturist position makes an absurdity of the God-breathed Scriptures.

By the way, did you notice the two polar opposite fates noted in the first passage above: "in Adam all **die**" but "in Christ all will be **made alive**"?

The third problem with this man's argument is that he appeals to "the orthodox view" rather than Scripture itself. Why? Because his position isn't supported by God's Word. As such, he has no other recourse but to appeal to man-made orthodoxy.

While 'orthodox' literally means "correct view," not all so-called orthodox views are biblical, which means they're not correct. Besides, appealing to "orthodoxy" raises the obvious question: Orthodox to whom? Does he mean the Catholic Church? If so, since when were they a sterling example of doctrinal correctness? If they were, there would've never been a Protestant Reformation. A true orthodox view is simply a thoroughly biblical view whereas an *un*orthodox view is *un*biblical.

' Cults Teach Destructionism—it doesn't Look Good '

Some have opposed the view of everlasting destruction on the grounds that it is adhered to (in one form or another) by various cultic or borderline cultic groups like the Jehovah's False Witnesses, the Seventh-Day Adventists,[28] Christadelphians and the Armstrongite sects.[29]

---

[28] Although the Seventh-Day Adventists are an evangelical sect, many consider them a "borderline cult" or even cultic because of their legalistic views regarding the Saturday Sabbath and Old Testament dietary laws, as well as their rigid allegiance to their prophetess, Ellen White, and their "all or nothing" mentality.

[29] Herbert W. Armstrong founded the Worldwide Church of God, a sect that was legalistic, exclusive and adhered to various strange doctrines (like Anglo-Israelism). In the mid-90s, a decade after Armstrong's death, this sect reformed to a more orthodox perspective, but there are numerous groups that splintered off—some adhering to Armstrong's teachings (e.g. the Philadelphia Church of God) and some not (e.g. the United Church of God). The main reformed group decided not to officially adopt the eternal torture doctrine; they instead left the

Some Christians I know—who openly admit that literal destructionism seems to be biblical—have pointed out that "it just doesn't look good" that cultic groups or borderline-cultic groups adhere to it in a flawed form.

I would counter that everlasting destruction is so blatantly obvious in Scripture that anyone who has high regard for God's Word and is not blinded by religious tradition is able to plainly see it. In short, **these groups adhere to literal destruction simply because they know how to read**.

We must understand that God is not prejudiced with knowledge and truth. *Whoever* humbly, honestly and diligently seeks knowledge and truth will find it, regardless of what sectarian tag they currently go by. Such groups as these have been able to see the biblical validity of destructionism because they stepped outside the blinding influence of religious tradition. Once this is done, the truth is clear for anyone who is literate.

Moreover, it is not a fair or valid argument to oppose a view simply because it is adhered to by a group with whom one objects. The groups mentioned above, and similar sects, have a high regard for Scripture (which is different than saying their theology is wholly sound); consequently, Evangelical Christians naturally agree with them on *many* things (e.g. adultery is a sin, prayer is important, etc.). Are we wrong on these issues simply because these objectionable groups adhere to them too? Should we reject what the Bible clearly teaches on these issues merely because these objectionable groups agree? Of course not. The argument holds no water.

Adherents of never-ending roasting resort to hollow arguments like this because of the abysmal lack of biblical support for their position. They're basically just **diverting attention** from the scriptural facts. It's nothing more than an **avoidance tactic** with the implication that people who adhere to literal destruction are

---

issue open, urging Christians to seek the matter out for themselves in the Scriptures and draw their own conclusions.

"guilty by association." This is fine as long as we understand that guilt by association works both ways. For instance, we could ludicrously argue that, since adherents of eternal torture believe in the immortality of human souls, and pagan religions and philosophies believe the same thing, then supporters of eternal torture are pagans. Or we could argue that, since false religions like Islam believe in eternal torture, then Christians who believe in eternal torture are false religionists as well. Need I go on?

Furthermore, we lose credibility with members of cultic organizations like the Jehovah's Witnesses and Christadelphians because of our official adherence to such doctrines as the immortality of the soul apart from Christ and eternal torture. Since members of such groups often know the Bible fairly well, it's impossible to ever convince them of these doctrines because they're not taught in the Bible. They reason that if we're wrong on these important issues, we're likely wrong on other doctrinal matters as well. We consequently close the door on rescuing them from the cults (or borderline cults) they're trapped in.

It goes without saying that members of cultic or borderline cultic organizations will be more open to more authentic forms of Christianity if we humbly admit that Church tradition has grievously erred in regards to the immortality of the soul apart from Christ and eternal torture.

Conclusion

This study concludes that the doctrine of eternal torment is a false teaching and only relevant to fallen angels. It was birthed from a satanic lie, is founded on a pagan view of human nature—that people possess immortality *apart* from Christ—and is perpetuated by sectarian allegiance to religious tradition rather than biblical truth. It is a stain on Christianity and a blasphemy to the just, merciful name of the LORD.

The doctrine of eternal torture is simply a gross mistake in Christian history. It's an error that can no longer be ignored or tolerated. We need to quit mindlessly believing unbiblical doctrines that misguided ministers peddle generation after generation and let the scriptural facts speak for themselves. It's time for Christians of all persuasions across the planet to rise up and boldly proclaim the biblical truth of everlasting destruction.

Yes, this must be done in a spirit of love and compassion, with much patience in face of the closed-mindedness or stubbornness of religious traditionalists. And, no, it's not an issue to break fellowship over (even though staunch advocates of eternal torment typically do this).

As we faithfully proclaim what the Judeo-Christian Scriptures plainly teach on human damnation (and human nature) the truth will expose the lie that the Church has wrongly embraced for so long. The doctrine of eternal torment needs to be put to rest in favor of what the Bible has always clearly taught on human damnation—**everlasting literal destruction with no hope of restoration or resurrection**.

Bibliography

Boice, James Montgomery. *Does Inerrancy Matter?* Oakland: International Council on Biblical Inerrancy, 1979

Buis, Harry. *The Doctrine of Eternal Punishment.* Philadelphia: Presbyterian and Reformed, 1957

Bullinger, Ethelbert W. *A Critical Lexicon and Concordance to the English and Greek New Testament.* Grand Rapids: Zondervan Publishing House, 1975

Catholic Encyclopedia, The. The Encyclopedia Press; First Edition, 1914

Constable, Henry. *Duration and Nature of Future Punishment.* London: Kellaway & Company, 1875.

Crim, Keith. *The Perennial Dictionary of World Religions.* New York: HarperCollins Publishers, 1981

Dake, Finis. *Dake's Annotated Reference Bible.* Lawrenceville: Dake Bible Sales, Inc. 1961, 1963

Fackre, Gabriel/Nash, Ronald H./Sanders, John. *What About Those Who Have Never Heard?* Downers Grove: InterVarsity Press, 1995

Fudge, Edward. *The Fire that Consumes.* Carlisle: The Paternoster Press, 1994

Fudge, Edward/Peterson, Robert. *Two Views of Hell.* Downers Grove: InterVarsity Press, 2000

Geisler, Norman L. *Encyclopedia of Christian Apologetics.* Grand Rapids: Baker Books, 1999

Geisler, Norman L. *Everything You Wanted to Know About Hell, But Were Afraid to Ask.* Discipleship Journal. May/June, 1995

Griesmeyer, Gary J. *The Myth of Everlasting Torment.* Gary Griesmeyer. Retrieved from www.wordonly.net, 2001-2003

Lindsey, Hal. *The Liberation of Planet Earth.* Grand Rapids: Harper, 1974

Kirkwood, David. *Your Best Year Yet!* Pittsburgh: Ethnos Press, 1996

LORD, The. *International Standard Version (ISV). Holy Bible.* Los Angeles: Davidson Press, 2013

LORD, The. *King James Version. Holy Bible.* Iowa Falls: World Bible Publishers

LORD, The. The NET Bible. Garland: Biblical Studies Press, 2006

LORD, The. *New American Standard Bible. Holy Bible.* Nashville: Holman, 1977

LORD, The. *New International Version. Holy Bible.* Nashville: Holman, 1986

LORD, The. *New International Version (Revised Version). Holy Bible.* Grand Rapids: Zondervan, 2011

LORD, The. *New King James Version Study Bible: Second Edition.* Nashville: Thomas Nelson, 2012

LORD, The. *New Revised Standard Version.* Holy Bible. Nashville: Nelson, 1989

LORD, The. *The Amplified Bible.* Grand Rapids: Zondervan, 1987

LORD, The. *Quest Study Bible: New International Version.* Grand Rapids: Zondervan, 2003

Lutzer, Erwin W. *One Minute After You Die.* Chicago: Moody Press, 1997

MacArthur, John. *The MacArthur Study Bible: New King James Version.* Nashville: Word Bibles, 1997

McFarland, Norman. *Delivered from Death unto Life.* Charlotte: A.C. Publications, 1974

McKee, John. *Why Hell Must Be Eternal, Part 2.* Retrieved from www.tnnonline.net, 2002 (a published book as of June, 2012)

Menzies, William W., and Stanley M. Horton. *Bible Doctrines: A Pentecostal Perspective.* Springfield: Gospel Publishing House, 1993

Pearlman, Myer. *Knowing the Doctrines of the Bible.* Springfield: Gospel Publishing House, 1990

Petavel, Emmanuel. *The Problem of Immortality* (translated by Frederick Ash Freer). London: Elliot Stock, 1892

Peterson, Robert A. *The Road to Hell... or the Path to the Cross?* In Covenant. June/July 1997

Pinnock, Clark. *Four Views on Hell: the Conditional View.* Grand Rapids: Zondervan, 1992

Reagan, David. *What Happens When You Die?* Lamb & Lion Ministries. Retrieved from http://www.lamblion.com/articles/articles_ eternity1.php, 1996-2016

Reagan, David. *The Nature of Hell: An Eternal Punishment or Eternal Torment?* Lamb & Lion Ministries. Retrieved from http://www. lamblion.com /articles/articles_eternity1.php, 1996-2016

Reid, Daniel. *Dictionary of Christianity in America.* Downers Grove: InterVarsity Press, 1990

Robertson, Pat. *Answers.* Nashville: Thomas Nelson Publishers, 1984

Scott, Miriam Van. *Encyclopedia of Hell.* New York: Martin's Press, 1998

Sheler, Jeffrey. *Hell's Sober Come Back.* U.S. News and World Report. 25 March 1991

Stott, John R. W., and David Edwards. *Essentials, A Liberal-Evangelical Dialogue.* London: Hodder & Stoughton, 1988

Strong, James. *Strong's Exhaustive Concordance.* Grand Rapids: Baker, 1991

Tertullian. *On the Resurrection of the Flesh* in The Ante-Nicene Fathers Volume 3:570 ed. Alexander Roberts and James Donaldson. Grand Rapids: Eerdmans, 1973

Vine, W.E. *Vine's Expository Dictionary of Biblical Words.* Cambridge: Nelson, 1985

White, Edward. *Life in Christ.* London: Elliot Stock, 1878

Wright, N T. *New Heavens, New Earth: The Biblical Picture of Christian Hope.* Cambridge: Grove Books limited, 1999

Fountain of Life

Teaching Ministry

(Psalm 36:9)

The mission of Fountain of Life is to **set the captives FREE** by **reaching the world** with the **life-changing truths of God's Word,** the **power of the Holy Spirit** and the **Awesome News of the message of Jesus Christ.**

We're calling Spiritual Warriors all over the Earth to partner with us on this mission!

Books by Dirk Waren:

The Believer's Guide to FORGIVENESS & WARFARE
Legalism Unmasked
HELL KNOW!
SHEOL KNOW!
The Four Stages of Spiritual Growth
ANGELS: Their Purpose and Your Responsibility
THE LAW and the Believer
What the Bible Really Teaches about FORGIVENESS
The Six Basic Doctrines of Christianity

www.ingramcontent.com/pod-product-compliance
Lightning Source LLC
Chambersburg PA
CBHW020501030426
42337CB00011B/190